Passive Income Freedom

"Ideas and strategies to become rich online, build different income streams and how to be financially free getting out of debts with online businesses, affiliate marketing, real estate, selling and renting products online."

Robert K. Grand

© Copyright 2019 by Robert K. Grand

All rights reserved.

This document is geared towards providing exact and reliable information with regards to the topic and issue covered. The publication is sold with the idea that the publisher is not required to render accounting, officially permitted, or otherwise, qualified services. If advice is necessary, legal or professional, a practiced individual in the profession should be ordered.

- From a Declaration of Principles, which was accepted and approved equally by a Committee of the American Bar Association and a Committee of Publishers and Associations.

In no way is it legal to reproduce, duplicate, or transmit any part of this document in either electronic means or in printed format. Recording of this publication is strictly prohibited, and any storage of this document is not allowed unless with written permission from the publisher. All rights reserved.

The information provided herein is stated to be truthful and consistent, in that any liability, in terms of inattention or otherwise, by any usage or abuse of any policies, processes, or directions contained within is the solitary and utter responsibility of the recipient reader. Under no circumstances will any legal responsibility or blame be held against the publisher for any reparation, damages, or monetary loss due to the information herein, either directly or indirectly.

Respective authors own all copyrights not held by the publisher.

The information herein is offered for informational purposes solely and is universal as such. The presentation of the information is without a contract or any type of guarantee assurance.

The trademarks that are used are without any consent, and the publication of the trademark is without permission or backing by the trademark owner. All trademarks and brands within this book are for clarifying purposes only and are owned by the owners themselves and not affiliated with this document

Table of Contents

Abstract 1
Why This Book 2
   Who is this eBook for? 3
Chapter 1 4
   Introduction 4
      What is Income? 9
      What is Passive Income? 11
   Is it a Conspiracy? 15
      Benefits That Come With Passive Income 16
      Financial Freedom 18
      Passive Income, Why, and How? 19
      Who Can Make Passive Income 32
Chapter 2 41
   What is Passive Income Freedom? 41
      Passive Income Freedom Mindset 49
      How to Make Your Money Attitude to Attract Wealth 58
   Passive Income Business Models 74
   How To Make Money With A Business Model 78
      Sell an eBook from a sales page. 78
      Sell a Kindle eBook. 79
      Sell an application 79
      Run a Website 80
   Differences between Traditional Business and Passive Income Business 80
      How To Create Wealth: Traditional Business Drawbacks
.... 80
Chapter 3 90
   Assets and Liabilities 90
   Assets and Liabilities: The Key to Wealth 93
      Relationship Between Assets and Liabilities: 95
Chapter 4 100
   Secrets to Repairing Bad Credit Score 100

Fixing Bad Credit Scores 102
Chapter 5 .... **106**
How to be Profitable 106
Tips To Increase Profits In Your Business 108
Chapter 6 .... **112**
Dropshipping Made Easy 112
   What is dropshipping? 112
   Steps to successfully start a Dropship company 115
   Five steps to successfully start a Dropship company .. 117
How To Find, Analyze And Sell Physical Products For Your Own Dropshipping Business 119
Chapter 7 .... **122**
Getting Started With Listing And Launching Products On eBay And Amazon 122
How To Source Products To Sell On eBay 124
   Understanding the Product 126
   How To Find Products To Sell Using eBay Sales Data 128
Launch Products Online to Increase Your Dollars 132
Chapter 8 .... **139**
What is Arbitrage? 139
What is Retail Arbitrage? 141
Tips for Retail Arbitrage on eBay 145
How to sell on Amazon with Retail Arbitration 147
Chapter 9 .... **149**
How You Can Work From Home 149
   Direct marketing 150
   Manage your own business 151
   Remember the returns at home 151
   Work at Home Scams 151
   Work at home for a "real" company 152
Tips For Working From Home 153
Chapter 10 .... **154**
How to Get Into Real Estate 154
How to Make Passive Income With Real Estate 157
Conclusion **159**

Abstract

It's possible to achieve Passive Income Freedom nowadays. The internet opens up endless possibilities for those who know how to catch them. You don't need much money or a particular skill, and anyone can achieve this following the right patterns with perseverance, dedication, and the right attitude.

This ebook will look over a few essential tips to becoming wealthy online and strategies to have passive income freedom. Moreover, it will look in-depth at online strategy and methods for making a quick buck, also will indulge in the specific qualities and knowledge required in the process of becoming rich online.

Before we can proceed, we must understand the meaning of the word "rich." What dictates the quantity of cash required to be classed as wealthy? This will be a non-public opinion and a query you have to answer for your quest for wealth, but if no longer, all can be mentioned inside the introductory part of this ebook. What stage of cash are you happy with?

Why This Book

Do you want more life, more money, more freedom, more safety, and more time for the activities you love?

If you are like me and hear another expert say that you have to earn some money by cutting the slats, you want to jump out the window. Please stop using frugality. Saving a few dollars, will it change your life? NO!

As you skimp on what you like, you see other people enjoying the financial freedom to do what they love, and they never must choose between paying bills and preserving money for their future or living a wealthy life.

When you are ready to stop saying "negative words" and start living the life you want, you must accept this financial truth: there's a limit to what you may store; however, there's no restriction to how plenty you may win.

You can spend hours a week on discount coupons to save a few dollars, or you can negotiate a salary increase that will save you thousands more per year for the rest of your life.

Yes, money is only one aspect of a rich life, but it can help us do the things we love and free ourselves from pursuing our dreams. I spent over ten thousand hours and a million bucks discovering and adapting the three best strategies to earn extra money - and I'll explain them in this ebook.

Who is this eBook for?

- If you want to ask for an increase and receive the commission that you deserve, This ebook monitors the techniques lots of college students have used to reinforce their earnings for lifestyles.
- If you want to create more money along the way or online—but don't recognize which to begin—this ebook is for you.
- In case you'd like to build your income the usage of competencies you already have, This ebook can help you get there.

Chapter 1

Introduction

Congratulations! You took step one toward making a massive change for your lifestyles, one which the majority by no means even don't forget.

This file is designed to introduce you to the wonders of passive income freedom and to demonstrate how simple a concept it's far to contain into anybody's life. That is now not approximately getting wealthy quickly (though it's feasible, that can happen).

Rather, it's an advent to clever business ideas that each successful entrepreneur is familiar with and takes advantage of. It's about doing the tough work as soon as it generates ongoing income in destiny.

The online community is growing a lot! As more and more individuals connect via the Internet, we have now become a truly worldwide community, and with almost 7 billion individuals around the globe, the Internet has become an amazing site for a variety of different reasons. You can meet new individuals, chat, learn fresh stuff, and remain up to date with what's going on around the globe. Most importantly, the Internet gives you an opportunity to make cash for many internet customers.

You've had to hear about the different ways to get wealthy online. One of the most popular techniques is to set up an online business. Many current companies are now expanding into the cyber globe. The primary reason behind this move is the enhanced market; instead of just selling to clients in your local region, internet companies can sell to the globe!

In addition, online businesses are cheaper and easier to handle: you don't have to pay for rent or utilities, and you don't have to worry about personnel expenses and loss of products. It's also very simple to begin your own company on the Internet. All you need is an idea of what to sell, a website, and you're prepared to go. With a bit of online marketing and advertising, you should be able to reach out to a broad spectrum of clients.

If you don't have a business idea, you can also become a member of multiple internet businesses. These businesses are selling a lot of products and services on the Internet. If you sign up as an affiliate, you will have the right to sell the company's products and advertise as their agent. In addition, you will receive instructions on how to develop your own website and conduct online marketing.

Getting rich online can also be different from buying and selling products. You can consider working online for an employer or company; The most common online job openings are writing articles and academic articles, internet marketing, data entry, and website design. If you have knowledge of these areas, you should easily find job openings online. Many employers and companies are looking for potential employees to help them with their workload, and if you are competent enough, you can be ready to win big!

Many people also earn money through blogs; By running your blog on a website, you can generate a movement of visitors on your website, and a lot of traffic is the only thing that online businesses want. If a company finds that your blog or website has a link with it, they might be interested in advertising on your website. Making money through blogs can be fun and easy if you write or they write something that you like. A growing number of people want to get rich online; check the internet today to search and try out potential job openings online; maybe you even love your online job more than your usual job!

When you hear the term "passive income," what image does this conjure in your mind? Do you really know what passive income is and why it is important to your financial future? If you have the slightest doubt, you'll want to read this whole ebook.

Passive income is just what it sounds like, but it is the income you receive without having to work in an active way to get it. This is in contrast to the income that most people have, which is an active income. Active income would be the money you get in your paycheck every month, for which you have to trade 40 hours of your time each and every week.

This is a very important distinction. Active income stops when you stop working on getting it. Your boss is not going to keep paying you if you stop showing up to work. If you sell things to make extra money, that money stops coming in when you stop selling. All active income streams are dependent on your actions.

Passive income, on the other hand, does not require ongoing effort. Often, you can do work once, and the income will continue to come in for months or even years without you having to do anything except maybe cash the checks.

You may be asking yourself why more people don't have any if this is such a great thing. The truth is that many methods of creating passive income require a lot of effort or discipline to create a passive income stream, and unfortunately, most people are not willing or able to get them started.

Many sources of income could be either passive or active, depending on how you set them up. Owning a business is a great example of this. There are several different ways of becoming a business owner, and they are as varied as buying stock in a public company and bootstrapping a start-up business.

If you have money and you are willing to do the research and learning involved in making a smart investment, buying stock may be the answer for you. Once you own the stock, you may receive dividend payments and enjoy any increases in the price of the stocks. This income continues without you having to do any further work. You may move from two folds to at least one fold to save some cents, or you could use the competencies you already ought to earn $ 1,000 consistent with a month (or more).

Creating your own business is another possible source of passive income, but for most business owners, this never becomes their reality. It can take a lot of patience to build up a business and hire the right employees and set up the right amount of automation to make it hands-off for you as an owner. But if you do so, you can enjoy years of income from this source without extra effort.

What is Income?

There are two main classes of income: Active and Passive.

- Passive Income

Income from activities In which an individual is not directly involved in, such as business, rental, royalty, or other enterprises. The best-selling author of "Rich Dad, Poor Dad," Robert Kiyosaki, for example, receives royalties for his book. He had spent some months writing the book once. His publisher publishes the book, and the bookstores sell his book. He oughtn't to be actively involved in selling his book but still secures an income regularly.

A person who has a franchise business also earns a passive financial gain through the gathering of franchise fees from his franchise. A good example is McDonald's. Ray Kroc, founder, and builder of the McDonald's Franchise System, created phenomenal success in the franchising business. At present day, there are more than twenty thousand restaurants in over 119 countries, and the franchise fees collected from them generated a huge passive income for the owner.

You could also make a passive income if you own the estate and decided to rent it. Robert G Allen, writer of the popular book title "Multiple Streams Of Income" is a strong supporter of property investments. He buys the property and then rent it. He earned a tremendous amount of passive income through the rental of his own properties.

- Active Income

This includes salaries, tips, commissions, and income from employment. In general, from businesses in which a person is actively involved.

The majority of the people live on Active Income. They're trading time for cash. A lot of people operate 8-5. And a lot of others need to work differents works to earn a fixed income. Most Active income earners hardly have enough money to retire, and they have to work all their life. They are bound by their job and deprived of their moment. They don't have time freedom, and they don't have financial freedom. Actually, they don't have freedom at all. As a matter of fact, when they stop working, their income stops.

Are you making money through Active or Passive incomes?

If you would want to be wealthy, you know that you must earn at least a Passive Income now.

What is Passive Income?

It can best be defined as income generated where the individual is not actively involved.

It can come in many forms ranging from dividend payments from stocks, rental income from property, or something as simple as a Gumball machine. This site has been designed to teach as many methods as possible on how to invest and build enough investments to start generating passive income and create a cash flow, which is ongoing in your everyday life without you having to do anything.

It is important that I stress here that I don't have any real get-rich-quick schemes to make a quick buck. The best way to describe the process is that of 'Wealth Creation.' With solid effort and motivation from the beginning, a business or investment can be set up to start generating an income for you with a little more work required from you once the hard work is done.

The Gumball machine example is a good one. Let's say I decide on purchasing a Gumball Machine and want to place it in a location where I know it will generate interest from the demographic mainly interested in Gumballs. A good example would be kids or, in some cases myself :)

I do the research and find that kids play area at a restaurant would be perfect; I make a deal with the owner that he can keep a certain percentage of the profits if he lets me place my machine there and helps me fill it up with gumballs if it's running low...(i know I'm lazy).

The best part is that I now have a passive income. If I sat on my butt all weekend watching DVDs while kids kept buying gumballs at the restaurant, I would still make money. This is known as a passive income stream, and it can be done in a number of ways, which will be explained throughout the site. The opportunities are endless, and there is no real limit to where your imagination can take you!

The most important part of a wealth creation strategy is making sure that you correctly use and develop what I like to call a financial mindset.

I know for a fact that not many people have it in them, but basically, it involves evaluating things based on how much money it can generate for them.

I definitely don't want to sound like a preacher because I absolutely understand that in life, not everything is about money, and there are far more important things.

Like I have mentioned before, the fact that you are on this site shows me you are exploring the concept of building wealth and creating a passive income, so I know that your a little financially minded already!

When I say financially minded, the best way I can put this is to pull an example from my favorite author Robert Kiyosaki.

If you see someone driving down the street in their brand new Porsche sports car with a girl under his arm and expensive jewelry all over him, would you consider him to be rich?

Well, maybe he is, but maybe he has taken out a loan to buy all his expensive gear and is borrowing money purely for his image.

In any case, one aspect is for sure the one's gadgets he spent money on are not going to generate any cash.

It is important though to remember that when buying something like a fancy car, watch, ring, whatever it might be, that it is purely for show and in most cases cannot build wealth.

Mostly in life, you will come across three different classes of people; those who can't afford things, those who can afford things and use their hard-earned salary to purchase them, and those who use their money to invest toward a wealth creation strategy and go without some of the things that are not necessities.

Now buying a luxurious item is not the wrong thing to do and in some cases, you should treat yourself, you need to do so in the knowledge that you are prepared to sacrifice a definite amount of money for that good.

Even a large house with a pool and spa and tennis court is nice and would be fantastic, but it is not an income-generating asset, and the money spent on the item is money, not earning you more money and should not be a part of a wealth creation strategy.

Is it a Conspiracy?

Actually, the passive income streams that we will teach you here are age-old principles. It is the Principle that a countless number of people throughout history have applied to make them very wealthy. More than a century ago, Andrew Carnegie said that: "Ninety percent of all millionaires became so through owning real estate." And to this day, there are many people still applying these principles and techniques to make a great deal of money.

Ironically, this knowledge is readily available today, but for some unknown reason, it is still not being offered as a subject in any education system. Dolf de Roos speaks of the "conspiracy theory" in his book titled "Real Estate Riches" as if we are purposefully being kept in the dark by the major financial institutions.

Your Dream of a Passive Income

Do you still dream? Do you think that a Passive Income is just a bad dream for you? You only received a specific small predetermined piece of the cake, and you will always stay poor because of that. You can clearly see that there is not enough for everybody. You believe that money doesn't grow on trees; that it takes money to make money; that the higher the return, the higher the risk, and you must study hard, get a good job, and work hard and you will be successful! It is much too risky to venture out of your comfort zone, and you keep on re-affirming these words, and therefore it will always be challenging to make money.

Benefits That Come With Passive Income

Among the most crucial inputs in any income-generating activity is time. Actually, this is the most attractive proposition of passive income. As a matter of fact, the investor could earn tidy sums with minimum effort as well as time. The definition of passive income does give the whole concept away since it is defined as referring to revenues that are made from one's investments against minimum work. There are many arguments on why passive income should be the priority of every person.

Saving time

The most apparent reason why there should be no convincing anyone to opt for passive income is the time aspect of the enterprise. In this scheme of things, one makes reasonable cash, yet the time spent is either minimal or not at all. This time that one has at their expense can then be used to engage in other activities such as leisurely pursuits or spending quality time with the family. However, everyone needs to understand that time is a crucial factor of production hence the need to realize how important a resource they save through passive income. Moreover, such time can be used to seek other income-generating enterprises, so helping to build a strong financial base. Such a process could sooner or later improve one's security and assures one of a long-term life of comfort. An exciting attribute that passive income does is to bring a new dimension into one's life. This is due to the freedom one enjoys choosing how to work, what to do, and if and when to work. The best part about it is that one continues to earn income even when they are not working. Passive income, therefore, gives one a break from the eight or nine hours a day, six or five-day working week.

Financial Freedom

Passive income allows a person to utilize the savings they have made to invest in the initial part. This phase is usually characterized by a very busy diary as one set in place the mechanism that will be relied upon to provide passive income. This could also help the individual to put good use of what would otherwise be considered idle money. In a way, passive income allows one to create more income than would have been possible by letting their savings stay in the bank. Compared to the interest the money would earn in a bank, this option is more productive by very big margins.

Since money is the greatest motivation for passive income, one will hardly be disappointed that they chose this option. It is a scheme that guarantees one a pay raise that does not involve haggling or pleading with one's boss. Passive income allows one to up their take-home package by simply increasing the income streams they rely on. Furthermore, the pay rise comes right away since the results are always immediate. Individuals are also constrained when it comes to increasing the amount of passive income they can generate. It is a limitless way of earning and expanding one's income flow. Finally, one gets a chance to make donations for worthy causes due to the freedom they enjoy from the passive income. With all these advantages, the only thing remaining should be to settle on a project that will start generating passive income.

Passive Income, Why, and How?

To become financially and personally successful:

The most important thing is to generate sufficient extra income from passive income streams. You then have enough time for your family, sports and other important things.

Passive- income streams will provide you with more money and the time to do the stuff you continually desired to do. Passive earnings are profits that are not at once related to your efforts. This means earning incomes without having to work for it directly.

You continue to earn money with passive income, regardless of whether you work or not. In the book Rich Dad Poor Dad, Robert Kiyosaki explains that to be in financial security, you have to develop passive income streams.

If you work and depend only on your own efforts and what you put into your work, you are always at risk. If you lose your job or income and you have no money coming in. If you have a passive income, it does not matter if you work or not; you will still receive your regular income.

To create a passive income, you have to put in a lot of time, money, and effort in the beginning. The best thing is to get the right opportunity to invest in that will pay you for the rest of your life.

Here are a few important facts on what you want in a passive income opportunity.

1. You need a good product or service that people want.
2. You want good, friendly, and personal support.
3. The system must be good and secure.
4. The compensation plan must be clear and worth the effort put in.
5. It must be easy and understandable.
6. It must be affordable to start.
7. You need people in your system. The more people in your system, the more money you will make.
8. You need a guarantee that it will work. It is also good if a "money back" option is offered.
9. You must make money soon and never pay more than what you make.
10. A good network is very important.

11. You do not want to sell products and recruit new people.
12. When people subscribe, you get income that increases your passive income.
13. The Internet and your website must do everything for you.
14. You need great marketing tools and methods.
15. The system must be automatic, and repetition must be easy.
16. Training, motivation, and support are important. This must be easily available from your website.
17. It should not be a get rich quick scheme, but your income should increase at a steady pace.
18. You should not spend more than 10 - 15 minutes per day to create your passive income.
19. A trial or testing period must be available for free.
20. There should be no risk.
21. Bonuses, incentives, and rewards should play an important role.

Bear in mind what the billionaire, John Paul Getty, said, I would alternatively benefit 10% from the efforts of one hundred guys running 10 hours each; then I must work the one hundred hours myself.

Such systems do exist. Depending on your level of online competency, you can choose the level where you want to start.

Sources of Passive Income

These days it is difficult to find sources of income. The gap between rich and poor is increasing. Some even say that if you work hard, you always have an income to survive. But how will you go about it if it is difficult to find a job? Even the rich struggle to maintain their income. However, this reduces the problem for some who know where to find sources of passive income.

First, let's define passive income. Passive income is a type of income from an investment. There are two types of income - assets and liabilities. We get an active income from the results of our work. Commissions, wages, tips, and service costs are the sources of active income. On the contrary, sources of passive income have different forms. Some popular sources are money itself, interest, dividends, sales, rent, etc.

Dividend

The dividend comes from the net income of a business enterprise. It is a shape of profit sharing and is greater common in the stock marketplace. When a company belongs to more than one person, the profit is distributed in proportion to the investment of each owner. Those owners are referred to as shareholders, and the sort of income is referred to as a dividend. The dividend can be money or shares. This is a cash dividend when the profit is distributed in cash by bank checks. And it's miles a stock dividend whilst it's far distributed as stocks or shares. As a source of passive income, the dividend is also appealing, specifically at some stage in the increase duration. Now not all groups give regular dividends. It's far vital to understand that stock selection determines your destiny earnings. If there are indications that the selected company is generating higher dividends, it may well continue. Most companies that consistently offer higher dividends are called income shares. The income shares cannot be large companies. Even some large companies cannot even generate substantial dividends because of their high operating costs. For example, not all shares are certainly one of the sources of passive income.

One of the many sources of income on the stock market is a 'source of income' that depends on the good industrial situation. For example, if the laptop industry is very attractive, any IT organization may be a candidate as a source of passive profits. This is that it is better to choose between these companies than to choose a very large company whose sector is experiencing economic problems. That is why a good source of passive income on the stock market is a good sector company.

Interest Earned

Earned interest is likewise one of the assets of passive income. Whilst we deposit our cash in a bank, our cash generates a hobby price. What is the interest? The interest rate is the percentage charged when we borrow money, and it is earned when we borrow. Despite the fact that we aren't always a lender, we also can earn these profits due to the fact the money that we've got deposited with a bank contributes to the quantity that the financial institution has lent to the borrowers. Of path, there's a situation earlier than we take into account our deposits as sources of profits.

We can consider that our savings are a source of passive income. This only happens when the interest is high and our down payment is large. Bank bonds or term deposits are examples of passive income. A savings account can also be one. Banks differ from each other due to their interest rates. To get an attractive income from banks, we must, therefore, choose the right bank and make a deposit at the proper time when the interest is high.

Rent

Passive sources of income are complex and numerous, but the simplest is rent or lease. Everyone knows, without any explanation, that income from renting or renting our property has proven to be a reliable source of income. If you have an extra house and plot or apartment, all you have to do is find someone who wants to occupy the place. Your passive income sources are not really your property here, but a reliable tenant who can consistently pay the rent and stay longer. The simplest consideration right here is the profile of your tenant. If your property is a commercial asset, you can rent it out to business people who set up a restaurant, a gas station, or a warehouse. The profile of your tenant is more credible here than that of the household. Tenants of trading land will certainly stay longer. This can be your concern because this type of investment is not liquid. It is a long-term investment. Yet, many of us will regard this as one of the best sources of income.

However, investment in transport services is hardly seen as one of the potential sources. The risk here is high. But if you are an ordinary person who owns one or two taxis, it is good to rent them, provided that you invest a little in the depreciation of your vehicles.

Sales

Buying and selling activities can be sources of income, depending on the items or goods you trade. The more trade you trade, the more income becomes passive. If we share small things, it is marketing and a good source of active income. But when we buy and sell cars, houses, and land, shares, and bonds, they are absolutely an excellent source of passive income.

Land

The land is the best source of income. It may not be rented on the grounds that time immemorial, it has been the maximum reliable supply of profits. In the past, fertile soil could produce crops, trees, plants, and grains without human intervention. Even cattle and poultry were fertile land products. All these things that the earth could produce were passive sources of income.

Equipment

In the country today, the equipment has become one of the major sources of passive income. The rice mill is the most popular material that you can use on the farm. During the harvest season, farmers pack their bags of rice at a purification plant. A rice mill owner receives a defined amount per bag. After the harvest season, the cash flow of the rice producers is much healthier than that of the farmers. The rice mill is hardly needed during this post-harvest season. However, other crops and grains require different types of equipment. For peanuts, the hulls and graders are at the front. Other types of agricultural machinery are agricultural tractors, mills, and dryers.

Even inside the town, equipment is one of the proper sources of passive income. The heavy system utilized in creation may be rented out to contractors and builders. In case you are an average man or woman, you should purchase a merchandising machine. A machine is being rented out. You will actually earn on your sold products. But it's considered a passive income because it's your machine that works for you. The printing press is the most popular and rented equipment in the city. It is a company and, at the same time, an investment.

We see that there are many sources of income. Instead of spending so much money on consumption, it is wise to invest in something that gives you an income to spend. Our active income is something that we must save, and our passive income is the income that we can spend. That is why our wise decisions are also sources of passive income.

Steps To Make A Passive Income

Many people are simply not happy with the income that they can currently generate. It doesn't matter if your career path is limited or if you have little time to make money; few are satisfied with what they can achieve. The use of passive income makes it possible to find new sources of income and to choose different ways. This source of income requires little from the responsible party and can be obtained by using the following methods to generate passive income.

Step One: Avoid using the solitary Persone

One of the first mistakes individuals make when trying to discover a new source of income is taking the loner. Most entrepreneurs believe that it is up to them to find the best solutions to meet their financial requirements and to find solutions to generate passive income. By taking on this isolated nature, you are actually limiting your options considerably because of your inexperience or lack of business relationships. Finding help from someone may seem counterproductive, but these resources can often provide ideas and solutions for generating extra income.

Step Two: Find the benefits of knowledge.

Almost everyone enjoys years of training, where she learns the basics of life. Whether you are a person who has completed the required minimum number of years of study or someone who has studied the lessons of higher education, one of the shortcomings of all systems is that they do not provide you with the knowledge of real-life to turn into wealth. This error limits the chances for a person who finds limitations on job expectations or the willingness to become an entrepreneur. Therefore, for every person, the second way is to earn passive income by looking for the benefits of knowledge.

Step Three: Use an established company

The last way to earn passive income is when you use an established business to achieve your income goals. Starting your own business is often the first source where entrepreneurs end up for ways to increase their income. It is much better to find a company that is looking for external resources to help it.

In this way, you can create your own work from home while using the benefits of a brand name, such as brand recognition and existing marketing tools.

When searching for ways to create a passive income, it is essential to take full advantage of the above three steps...

Passive Income Streams

We would like to show you in these articles how you can realize your dreams to achieve a position in your life where you can stop working for money but instead get the money to work for you! Contrary to the conventional approach to work for your money during your working lifetime and invest that in assets, we will show you a simple yet very effective method whereby you can earn passive income streams, working smart and not hard. And frankly, you would be thrilled to learn that you can make money without really having to "work" for it in the usual sense.

Generate a Passive Income with Buy-to-Let Properties

We sincerely hope to empower you through these series of articles, which will give you effective and valuable guidance so that you can secure a passive income stream through buy-to-let properties, releasing you from the necessity of "work."

We will give you, through these articles, all the information you need to build for yourself a passive income that will satisfy your needs and more.

We will teach you all the strategies that you need for a successful buy-to-let, residential property investment business:

- You will earn a passive income so that you can enjoy an early retirement
- You will be able to experience the joys of being an Asset-Owner versus an Income-Earner
- You will learn the power of gearing
- Escape the web of debt

Just Do It!

Unfortunately, regardless of what we want to teach you here, the majority of people reading these articles will stick with what they are doing now and not do anything about their financial problems. According to the Pareto principle, eighty percent of people are so deeply entrenched in their way of living, beliefs, and upbringing that they will do nothing to improve their circumstances. No matter how easy it can be!

That leaves twenty percent of the population that will, in some way, react to these teachings. Which one will you be part of? The twenty percent or eighty percent!

Who Can Make Passive Income

Don't let anyone fool you; building passive income streams is hard work.

If your motivation for passive income is an escape, you will probably fail. Passive income is the fuel needed to extend the life you want to live in and requires much hard work, especially in advance. If you are looking for an easy way out, you will probably give up before you go far.

It's important to create money and passive income around things you are passionate about to fuel success. Don't assume you can escape it by growing streams of passive profits. It might not work. However, in case you are willing to place within the time to study and the work required, anyone at any age can begin making passive earnings now!

Students

Any student is given assignments, papers to write, projects to do. Particularly on the university and excessive college level, why not take one of your courses and turn it into a passive income stream?

For example, if you are a health enthusiast and go to school to become a health coach and especially like this type of work, you can expand your service with something like an online course, an ebook or a website that allows you to have a Passive value that you can offer to people, even when you are not available, to help them individually. Or have not yet graduated. As long as you are honest and base it on love, this is a great way to make passive income before and after graduation.

Why not? You are learning things to get you certified or trained. Explain to your audience what your blog is about; you are an aspiring health student, what you learned and are learning, and package some of the information up to sell. Or, at the very least, create a ton of free valuable content, which will drive tons of free traffic to your website and then monetize the site by putting up ads or use affiliate marketing for useful products and services. This could assist you to earn passive income. Passive earnings is a side impact of imparting passive cost.

You could then expand your services after you did graduate and add another stream of income by providing person-to-person health coaching services. You have created a "job" while you were in school. You have already created your own virtual "health center/office" with lots of clients who trust and worth your opinion and who would most likely be elated to have some of your coaching services.

Now tell me this isn't much smarter than going to class, writing papers, and doing nothing more. Then when it comes time for graduation, you get to start fresh by printing up business cards and knocking on doors. Or better yet, polishing up that dreadful resume (with probably zero experience besides serving food because you were in school) and applying for jobs.

Yes, it will be hard work and take a lot of energy to write your assignments over into ready-friendly content. Or experiment with healthful recipes and create an eBook, but in the long run, this sounds like a much more intelligent plan. Depending on how hard you work, you may even generate enough passive income to come out of school debt-free, now that sounds like a winner!

Parents

For all you parents out there, they're probably just doesn't feel like enough time in the day to get everything done. How are you supposed to create a passive stream of income on top of it all?

My suggestion is to break it down. Write one article when the kids go to sleep every night, at least 300 words. Your topic/niche can be very simple. Don't over-analyze this.

So you are a mother who wants more healthy recipes using fresh ingredients? Turn your passive income stream into something you already want to learn how to make healthy recipes using fresh ingredients.

Let's do this together. If you go to the google keyword tool and type in "healthy recipes," you can see that there are over 1,500,000 search queries a month with a medium competition level. That's a pretty broad topic of winning over, and the chances are that you won't rank very high with Google trying to win that keyword/niche.

There are more than 60,000 search queries per month with low competition and almost 12,000 search queries per month for "good salad dressings" with low competition. So if you've produced your site around healthy salad and tasty salad dressing recipes, you could have a potential of 72,000 visitors per month! That's a lot of traffic, and the choices for monetization are infinite.

As a mother of two, for example, you want to create a website/blog to earn a passive income with healthy salad and salad recipes. You, therefore, commit yourself for up to 300 days during the following 365 days (one year). You learn, research, and make a recipe for a healthy salad or salad dressing to give to your family, and then make an appropriate article/recipe to add to your website with a beautiful photo. You use the Google keywords, then after 300 recipes, you take the top 50 and package it in an eBook that you sell for $ 15.

Let's say you're on Google's front page now because you're beginning to master the niche keywords "healthy salads" and "healthy salad recipes," and your monthly traffic is 20,000 visitors. Now let's say you've got a 2% conversion rate on your eBook of "50 Best Healthy Salads and Dressings" that you're selling for $15. That implies you'll be selling around

400 ebooks in a month, and at $15 each, you're making around $6,000 a month of passive earnings! The best part of it is that you have to know something that you wished anyway... how to feed your family healthy, and you're helping other families do the same thing, but now you're getting paid for it.

I am positive it became a ton of labor in advance, you'll have instead rested after the youngsters went to bed and watched a movie with the hubby instead of writing approximately vinegar and oils, but it was worth it, wasn't it? Hard work upfront pays off!

Both groups of individuals, students and parents are very BUSY! But it can be achieved, and it ought to be done. You don't have anyone to blame, but if you don't attempt, it's pretty stupid not to do that. Take a look at your niche and create a website to begin earning passive income.

Passive Income - Language Abuse?

In a sense, passive income is unsuitable because nothing prevents you from being responsible for a group of income-generating assets. Whether it is a real estate portfolio or a company that you own and manage, it is seldom or never really passive. You must be involved in asset management at a certain level. However, it is passive in the sense that it does not require your daily direct involvement.

To get rich, consider leveraging/passive income by increasing the size and level of your network instead of simply increasing your skills/expertise. Smart people can spend their time collecting diplomas and certificates. However, the rich spend their time collecting enterprise cards and building relationships!

Residual Income = A Form Of Passive Income

Residual income is a form of passive income. The two terms are often used interchangeably. However, there's a diffused important difference between the two. Residual income is actually the income that is generated from time to time by the work that is performed as soon as you receive recurring payments that you receive long after the original product/first sale. The remaining income is usually expressed in specific amounts and paid at regular intervals. Here is an example of remaining income: -

- The fees/income from the publication of a book.
- The commissions for the renewal of financial products that are paid to a financial adviser.
- Rental of a home.

- The revenues that are generated in marketing networks at multiple levels.

Using the resources of others and the money of others

The use of the resources of others and the money of others is an essential ingredient for generating passive income. The money from others saves you time (a key factor that limits the income earned when creating wealth). In a sense, using other people's resources gives you time. When it comes to raising capital, companies that generate passive income usually attract the most money from others. Indeed, it is usually possible to closely estimate the return (or the risk) that you can expect from passive investments. So banks, etc., will often finance passive investment ventures. A good business plan studied and prepared by a very good management team will generally attract so-called "angel investors" or even venture capital funds. And real estate can often be purchased with a small down payment, with most of the money being borrowed from a bank.

Tax Benefits Of Passive Income

Passive income investments often offer the most favorable tax treatment if they are well structured. For example, companies can use their profits to invest in other passive investments (such as real estate) and thereby benefit from tax deductions. And real estate can be 'traded' for larger real estate, whereby taxes are postponed indefinitely. The passive income tax will vary depending on the personal tax bracket of the individual and the corporate structures used. By way of illustration, we can state that an average tax of 20% on passive investments would be a reasonable assumption.

Chapter summary:

It is not for nothing that passive income is often regarded as the holy grail of investment and the key to long-term wealth creation and wealth protection. The main advantage of passive income is that it is a recurring income, usually generated month after month without much effort on your part. Building wealth and getting rich should not be about withdrawing the least effort from your own energy, resources, and money, because there is always a limit to what you can do. Exploiting the actual generation and using passive income is a crucial step on the road to wealth creation. Begin this part of your journey to creating wealth as soon as the human is possible, that is, right now!

This will bring us to the next chapter on what Passive Income Freedom means.

Chapter 2

What is Passive Income Freedom?

Have you ever thought of what to do if you never had to work for money again? For many people, this idea comes to mind only when they think about winning the lottery or things like that, and, unfortunately, that is a real shame. If more people had an understanding of passive income and the effect it could have on their financial future, they probably would not even entertain playing the lottery.

Financial freedom is a term that can be easily misunderstood, but it isn't complicated. Being financially free means that you have enough passive income to allow you to live the lifestyle of your choosing. This means that you would never have to get up and go to a job you hate every morning to be sure that your mortgage or rent gets paid.

The key to this is passive income, which is income that you earn without having to work for it actively. That doesn't mean that there is no work involved, just that once the work is done, it will continue to pay you for a long time into the future, whether you put any additional effort into it or not.

To understand this better, you may need to see an example that fits into your own life. If you rent an apartment, every month, you write out a check to a landlord. From your perspective, this is an expense, but from the landlord's perspective, it is income.

The landlord bought the building and then probably hired a management company to take care of repairs, rent collection advertising, and all the other details that need to be attended to each day. He had the expense and effort of finding and buying the building, but now he earns an income from this for as long as he continues to own and rent out the apartments.

If you are thinking to yourself that you couldn't afford to buy a building or hire a management company, then maybe this isn't the passive income stream for you. Another example of passive income is interest payments. The most well-known example of this would be a savings account at your bank, however, there are many ways you can gain more interest than these pays.

Of course, earning $100 each month in passive income will not give most people financial freedom, so how is it possible for the average person to get there? Simple, you need to find ways to develop many different passive income streams, and then take that money and reinvest it in other passive income streams until you build up enough streams to support your chosen lifestyle.

It does take work, discipline, and if you are starting out small, patience to get to the point of financial freedom. If this sounds like too much for you, ask yourself how much discipline it takes to get up every day and get yourself to a job you don't like. Or how much work you put in once you get there. Don't you think you can do at least the same for yourself as you do for your boss? Surely you're worth the effort.

Are You Looking For Passive Income Freedom?

How many are needed? Why do we always have to think about money or our income in terms of what is enough to live a good life? Nature is considerable, and there's more than sufficient for every person to enjoy. If you look at a fruit tree, it is full of fruit - not just "enough" to feed you, your family, or your friends. If we are part of nature, why do we constantly think of winning "enough" to feel comfortable and not to think of abundance?

Assume huge these days and see if we can destroy through our limiting beliefs approximately cash and profits and unlock our excessive income/excessive achievement mentality.

There are four main points to change your income or money mentality:

Point 1: Breakdown the need to work hours for dollars

Many starting entrepreneurs leave their jobs to start a business or start an extra business to earn more. They think their new company would give them more freedom; however, they discover that they're nevertheless running difficult and calculating cash in hours to greenbacks.

On the other side, individuals in non-entrepreneurs employment discover themselves unhappy because their incremental earnings over time are not enough for them to live the life they want to lead. Their challenging work overtime does not offer them the money they need to retire and live off their savings. The stress and pressure of work and the maintenance of work only contribute to the sensation of insufficiency.

How are you going to break the cycle of working hours for dollars and make profits that will allow you to live the lifestyle you want?

To answer this question, you need to know the notion of being a "businessman lifestyle." A lifestyle entrepreneur produces an enterprise that revolves around the lifestyle they want to live in. They create cash through a powerful knowledge of and execution of passive income policies.

The question that you must ask at the moment is:

"What kind of lifestyle do I love to live in? Does my current career (or company) provide me with the means, and can I live that way? What else do I have to change?"

Write the answers in your journal if you may. You will be pleasantly surprised by the answers you provide.

Point 2: Stop being and feel undervalued - Assess your true potential

If you're a company owner, a freelancer, a solo entrepreneur, or just someone who's making the shift from a job to being your boss, you understand as well as I do, working hard is essential for achievement. By the way, hard work without clarity is going to get you nowhere. Without a clear strategy for your life and business, clear profit targets, and a clear picture of how you can do it, your perseverance won't pay off.

Is that why many people don't have any clarity? Clarity involves three stuff:

1. Understanding your purpose: what do you want to do in this universe?
2. Understanding Your Value: What distinctive abilities do you have that would help you make a difference in this universe?
3. Understanding Your Potential: What unique capacity do you have to make this occur, and how?

I will give you an example. My goal in my company is to create effective company leaders who have a strong effect on their communities. My distinctive abilities lie in communication, the creation of workshops, and online marketing. I use this to interact and offer our content to our customers, to create my weekly Inbox Magazine, and my internet coaching programs.

It all starts with assessing your true growth potential – if your present job or business isn't using your best life-creation skills, you need to step back a bit and look for the right direction.

Point 3: Exponential Growth Focus Many individuals concentrate on linear growth, a slow, incremental rise in what they've earned throughout their life. On the other side, successful individuals practice exponential growth. They generate various streams of revenue that allow them to grow in leaps. It's exponential growth that provides you financial freedom. It's precisely what produces real abundance.

How are you creating exponential growth? This contributes to key 4, which is the extension of this key to achievement.

Point 4: Find a leveraged system that gives you passive income through multiple channels

Success has never been random. It is a continuous method of innovation and development. You need to discover the correct banking system to provide you with the instruments and the basis to generate the exponential growth you're looking for. So, the most significant blueprint that we can offer you today is this:

1. Rely on a leveraged scheme that can offer you exponential development–find an internet marketing and internet company platform that can automate your company.
2. Learn how to generate various streams of income through this scheme by completely utilizing your distinctive abilities and your full potential. Once you understand and see success with a single product or service in your project, you can recreate a system for various products and services (thus creating multiple revenue streams).

Important note: although I say that you create multiple income streams, you must bear in mind that you must first succeed in a project, product, or service before you can diversify. Don't distract yourself with too many projects when you start.

3. Create passive income strategies and avoid hours of work. If you want to consult, or follow individual sessions or want to work on a practical project, then do this absolutely. But do not forget to create additional channels that also provide you with a passive income. Passive income strategies help your company make money even if you are not physically

present. Some examples can automate online programs for your business, download books and PDFs, take advantage of affiliate marketing (resale programs created by others), or simply by asking your affiliates to sell your program around the world.

If you decide to do this, a change in your SPIRIT INCOME and your INCOME strategies will help you increase your income capacity. It's always up to you to choose smart business and economic growth.

Passive Income Freedom Mindset

Have you ever wanted to have a company that allows you to generate passive income and gives you the freedom to live the kind of lifestyle of your dreams?

Most people with this choice would do it! But they have one thing that goes against them, and, surprisingly, they are their own limiting beliefs.

No matter what kind of education we're all programmed to have our faith set, there are things you're taught what you can and can't do that are strengthened regularly through schools, media, workplaces, and friends. For instance, rich people get richer and poor people get poorer. Yes, that's true, but what are the reasons for that?

The wealthy and successful have a different mentality than the ordinary working man or woman, and this is nothing to do with superiority or intelligence.

They have the right way of thinking; if they discover a hurdle in front of them blocking their path, they find a way around it if even they run into a wall to discover a method to scale it.

They have a solution-driven mentality that has been honed over time. It is not something that they were born with.

The Successful Mindset

The brain works in much the same way as a muscle; if the body is exposed to a rigorous work out with the right diet and required periods of rest, the body reacts by getting stronger, resulting in a firmer muscle tone; likewise, if the mind is engaged to situations out of the normal comfort zone, it will quickly adapt to deal with whatever environment that it is exposed to.

The successful wealthy is by allowing themselves to be in a pressurized environment, and be psychologically acclimatized to these high-pressure situations. As a result, they are better equipped mentally to take stress.

Through trial and error, the experiences gained under demanding conditions build resistance, helping make the mind stronger and more resourceful.

The successful entrepreneur also possess other qualities such as

- Planning Ahead
- Anticipating change and being in a state of readiness
- Investing in their business at the right time
- Leadership qualities
- Unafraid to take a calculated risk
- Excellent communication skills

Taking Positive Action

The capacity to alter and adapt their company and then to see the findings of their actions reinforces their ability to do the correct thing. Therefore action is equal to success, and this action continues to result in further accomplishment.

Forming a Definite Desire to Succeed

It all starts with the burning desire to become someone, to do something great, to change things, to have something, to help others.

All successful people have strong intentions and ambitions. So change your goals into clear statements and turn them into a clear desire.

A desire in itself gives you confidence in what you do because you now have a goal, a goal, and a direction.

Let us now focus on the most important elements of a certain desire.

1. Belief

"No one is ready for one thing until he thinks he can attain it. The state of mind must be a conviction, not just a hope or a wish. Openness is essential for faith. A closed mind does not inspire faith, courage, and conviction."

Hill points out that hope and desire are not strong enough to describe what is needed to succeed. What he calls a determined desire is so powerful that it can change your reality.

Strong conviction is fundamental and very important if you want to improve. It is linked to certainty.

"There is a quality that one must possess to win; it is the precision of the goal, the knowledge of what one wants, and a burning desire to possess it."

If you do not believe in yourself or your ideas, you will never let others believe in these ideas, and you will never see your wish come true.

2. Faith

Faith is the eternal elixir that gives life, power, and action on the impetus of thought. Faith is the only antidote known to fail.

You must not only believe in your goals and desires, but you must also be able to trust that everything will be fine and that everything will go as smoothly as possible.

Sometimes it can be very difficult, given the many distractions around us. But still, have faith! Believe that it is possible and that it will finally be the case. Have faith in yourself and in your actions.

The universe is created to work with you, not against you, as many people think. And if you have a strong desire, he will do everything to help you get it.

Faith is just a state of mind that can be induced or created through confirmation or repeated instructions to the subconscious mind, according to the principle of self-suggestion.

3. Determination

"The determination of a man's bulldog, his persistence in defeating a single desire, was intended to override any opposition and to give him the opportunity he was looking for."

Perhaps you have seen people so focused on their goal that they leave nothing behind and don't stand in the way of others, give up on what they did before and only focus on what leads them to the life they want to lead.

Many people see them as crazy, but usually, those who criticize are so common that any change and passionate person with a state of mind turned to success seems strange to them. They cannot understand why these people act that way and why they believe so badly in something that could one day become a reality or not.

Obsession can be a good thing. This is not well accepted, but it does not mean that you forget everything that is important in your life. Instead, it means that you want what you want and that you focus on it every day.

It means that you do not let others keep you from your dream (prepare for such people); you do not let the mistakes of the past influence your actual behavior and thinking. It means being focused on what you really desire and constantly trying to get closer.

4. Visualize success

See your success before you really are. Look around you. You see this reality as it is. Everyone can do it, and that's why it stays the same. But if we change what we see unconsciously, if we permit our minds to consider that the whole thing around us is higher, we're happier, we've everything we need, this is where our reality looks.

Visualizing is seeing your desire come true, imagining in detail what you want, thinking that you succeed, feeling yourself too. The change that you want to see is what it really makes.

To hope and wish that something is not enough, you need to have this preference and visualize it each day. It ought to be robust, and the picture must be clean that allows you to reach your subconsciousness.

5. Affirmations

"The repetition of the confirmation of commands to your subconscious mind is the only known method for voluntary development of the movement of faith."

Claims are statements, mantras that we must repeat until we truly believe in them. They must be:

- Positive;
- Short - so that they can be absorbed better by the mind;

Repeated every day - you may do it inside the morning while you awaken and within the night time earlier than you go to sleep. The more you read, say out loud, and repeat, the better the result.

This is the principle of self-suggestion. Repetition is a key factor because it will always make you think of your goal and not let you lose focus.

"If you repeat the famous Emil Cove formula a million times," I get better and better every day. "Without combining emotion and faith with your words, you will not experience any desired outcome."

That is why visualization + repetition + emotion + faith is the best combination for success.

Imagine how you'll feel when you'll reach your goal and be as more specific as you can do; it will be easier for you to accept that it is possible in all ways.

Confirmations can be repeated (preferably out loud) as part of your morning routine, during meditation, or in front of a mirror. For the best result, you need to be relaxed, focused on what you say, be confident, and really believe it.

Let us continue with the development of a money mindset.

How to Make Your Money Attitude to Attract Wealth

Have you ever wondered why the poor generally stay poor while the rich get richer? The explanation is simple and directly related to their attitude to money.

In money matters, there are two types of people.

Those in the first group do not have enough but do not take the initiative to find ways to do more. Instead, these people are negative towards everyone who is rich. They accuse rich people of an easy life, but at the same time, they show signs of jealousy and hatred. This prevents them from having a balance in their lives and ultimately becomes miserable.

When it comes to money, they think it's a bad thing. They complain that they never have enough but do not want to work hard to start a company or participate in someone else's project because it takes a lot of time, and there is always a chance of failure.

However, one of the most important laws of life is that desire in combination with action is the turning point of all achievements.

This means that a man who sets big goals must want to achieve them. Such a desire comes from within and is what motivates and helps to overcome obstacles such as doubts and fears.

It is not surprising that the poor remain poor throughout their lives. Their attitude toward money is wrong; their approach is also not the right one. And those who don't always do something to realize a dream don't deserve to be rich.

Let's look at the second group of people based on the kind of mentality they share - the rich.

Having an Abundance Mentality

All rich people and successful business people have a number of things in common. First, they regard money as a good thing.

When respected and properly spent, they can offer enough for their loved ones, enable them to live a pleasant life, and enable them to develop their activities and contribute to the world.

So they welcome the money into their lives.

They see their bank account grow in their heads before something really starts to happen. That is how they accept the abundance that comes their way.

Such an attitude towards money makes you an initiative.

Wealthy people don't stay in bed all day or spend their time in their yachts.

We are not talking about celebrities and heirs.

I describe strategic, determined, hard-working, and persistent men and women in history and today who think they are great, seize opportunities when they knock on the door, and get closer to the lifestyle they planned every day.

They do not turn away from the ultimate goal. They create positive images in their mind about money.

They have needs and must collect the amounts needed to satisfy them.

They also differ from the poor in the way they talk about money.

They show respect, use powerful words, are not afraid to say they will have a lot in a year, and are even enthusiastic about all the new doors that this financial freedom will open for them.

In short, your mentality determines your future wealth.

If you have a certain state of mind, you will accept that you have limits and that you are not destined to have a lot of money. On the other hand, a person with a growth mentality will know that it is only a matter of time, that it increases your vibrations, follows your intuition, that it has a focused approach, and, possibly, that it attracts abundance.

Decision combined with courage.

So how can we change our mentality and become prosperous?

The success technique for earning a lot of money is no secret. It starts with a clear desire, but in the end, it is only important to know what decisions to be made and whether you have acted or not.

When most people have to make a choice, they have doubts about it. And doubt is a big mental barrier that prevents you from thinking logically and leads to confusion.

You can think about something for days and postpone the final decision until it is too late to do something.

The smarter approach to decision making is to choose an option and believe so much in yourself that you will make the best of it. It is about resourceful, determined, and courageous.

Whether you want more money, career success, a better social life, and more constructive relationships, or it is always the winner who wins.

It is also what helps you to develop a positive attitude toward money.

Carol Dweck, an American psychology professor at Stanford University, became very popular with a book called "Mindset."

In this book, she examines a fantastic theory about the two most important types of mentalities developed during their lifetime, which are the main reason for their success or absence.

People with a certain state of mind are convinced that our options are limited and that there are very few things that we can achieve in our lives.

Unfortunately, this usually prevents them from continuing their education after school, learning new things, or setting larger goals.

They simply believe that this is all useless because their current level is the highest they can achieve in life.

If you consider it, you can understand these people in your environment and see the signs of mediocrity and inability to change or improve.

On the other hand, what helps the world evolve are people with a growth mentality.

They are the best performing, the successful entrepreneurs, the hard workers of any company being promoted and reaching the peak of their careers, the students who exceed their teacher's expectations, and more.

They think that our powers are unlimited and that failure is not an option when it comes to determination, initiative, and a learning process.

These people do not differ physically or mentally from the other group. They are not born with a talent, have no specific skills, and are not smarter.

But they want to learn and grow every day. They look for opportunities, put extra effort into it, develop a powerful mind at a young age, and use it effectively later to realize their dreams.

If you are not there yet, don't be discouraged. You can improve your state of mind, change your attitude to money, create an abundant mentality, and put on whatever you want.

How? Well, to start, stop counting on your luck and look no further for an easy option. Even if there is one, it is unlikely that it will guide you where you are going.

The big transformations start small and start inside.

Take the time in the coming days to have a conversation with yourself. Determine what you need and what you're inclined to sacrifice to get it.

Big dreams should not scare you.

Becoming a millionaire is not impossible. But that also starts with changing your attitude towards money and getting rich first.

To create abundance in your life and to have a positive attitude toward money, you begin to appreciate what you already have.

There are more than you think. Take a look around.

Start every day by thanking people around you who love and support you for the house you live in, the qualities you have, the challenges you have overcome, and the opportunities that are available to you.

This exercise helps you to get out of negativity, and you will see that it is already abundant in your life.

You will no longer feel that something is missing. Instead, you will become richer by embracing gratitude. Once you do that, you can concentrate on getting more of everything you have.

As we know, tastes taste. If you feel so happy about the good things in your life, you'll get more out of it every day.

Then the time comes to put into practice what Napoleon Hill preaches: be brave within the proper direction, say sure to opportunities, start new tasks, take dangers, take initiatives and create your own happiness.

As you do this, you may want to strengthen your conviction when despair and the fear of failure return. And they go at some point. But with a strong mentality and a positive vision of the future in mind, you can manage them effortlessly.

Life is Beautiful, and you can have a lot of things if you know how to put them on. Believe in yourself and your skills, grow up with new experiences, more knowledge, and challenge your limits.

If you want something serious enough, this must be the last thing you think about before you go to sleep at night and the first thought that will consume your mind when you open your eyes.

This is how you can increase your energy and start bringing everything that has the same vibrations that will help you get closer to this goal.

Make sure you enjoy yourself during your journey to the ideal lifestyle and wealth-building.

The idea that you are doing something for yourself and creating a better future should be enough to keep you motivated and on the right track.

However, it does not have to be a daunting process. Enjoy every day you get while at the same time focusing on the end goal.

What can you do today to change your attitude to money and create an abundance mentality?

What to do and not to get rich

Most people say they want to be rich, but what they actually do is different.

They keep working and complain about their average work, comparing their lives with those of rich people, looking for simple ways to get money faster.

In their free time, they practice unproductive activities, spend time with other average people, and talk about random events and things instead of ideas.

Those who are about to get rich, however, get the best out of every minute of their day, note and seize opportunities and hurry while keeping in mind their long-term vision.

You know what kind you are, but whatever the situation, you can reverse the situation and begin your journey to the dream life of today.

And it is not only where the money is, but wheretrue satisfaction, meaning, and passion are hidden.

These are the best ways to get rich:

1. Change your attitude to money.

The poor generally stay poor while the rich get richer. The most important difference is inside. In short, wealth consists of developing a powerful state of mind instead of being part of the crowd.

Firstly, keep in mind that money won't bring you luck. It will be the way to live a more luxurious life, try everything, visit all the places in the world and touch millions of people.

So you have to set very specific goals and then look for the money to reach those goals.

So, understand that time is greater critical than cash. Some people have thousands and thousands of dollars in their bank account but cannot save a minute of their day without forgetting a spontaneous trip to another country.

It means they don't have anything. And this is not the kind of empire that you want to be. Then change your consumption behavior:

- stop buying and start selling;
- reduce expenses to the absolute minimum until you start earning income;
- invest in your knowledge and skills - they are invaluable and always bear fruit;
- money should be spent if you have it - so no credit, loans, etc.
- only spend if there is a reason, not just because you have money in your pocket;
- evaluate your money, and you will spend it.

2. Change your environment.

If you really want to get rich and soon have a better lifestyle, you have to do it differently:

- stop spending time with the poor - they only talk about average things, and it affects you more than you think;
- find passionate visionaries, executioners, and risky
- takers;
- find mentors;
- do not listen to opponents;
- do not share your goals with people;

- do not use the information made for the masses; carefully choose what you put in your head and read, for example, what rich people read.

3. Stop doing something that doesn't make you rich.

80/20 your life, but this time more strategic. Eliminate everything that does not increase your income; you help build relationships with the right people or open new doors. And make more than 20% that brings you closer to your final goal.

This will greatly facilitate the daily decisions. Before you make a choice, ask yourself this question: "Will this help me become rich?" And act according to the answer.

It simplifies life if you think about it and allows you to make continuous progress.

If you are not sure what you will never make rich, here are the most important ones:

- Spend money that you don't have.

Taking a loan or something that is close by is actually spending money that you don't have. And there is no way that it can help you become richer in the future. In fact, you reduce your chances of becoming a day rich.

So please, don't spend money you don't have.

- A job will never make you rich.

Indeed it is the exact opposite: if you work in a job, you enrich someone else. You also don't use all your potential; you are bored and depressed; you perform random tasks; you are not productive and probably in a bad environment.

But that too is part of the system. Of course, you must start with a normal job before you become independent. You just have to pay the bills while working on something you believe on the site and hoping to take advantage of the power of the internet to build something of yourself and free yourself from 9 to 5.

- A different diploma does not make you richer either. More degrees can be bonus points to get a better job. However, your plan is to get out of the rat race and seize opportunities, work hard, stay focused on an end goal, and build something that people are willing to pay.

You won't get there with a different diploma. It means more money and more years of your life spent on education, including many things you will never need in real life.

Invest in books instead, contact influencers in your niche, find mentors, talk to potential clients about the product you are trying to make.

It is a matter of self-study and experience. Be selective and learn throughout life. Make mistakes and try a different approach next time until you succeed.

It is 100 times better than any degree.

– Too many dreams.

You will have to raise your standards in terms of what is possible. But that does not mean that you have to get lost in dreams.

Instead, keep your head in the clouds, but keep your feet on the ground.

Dream big, but turn them into goals and act daily to get close to them.

– Spend time with the arms.

Communicating with the same people you have always known does not change anything. Instead, do not listen to them; do not discuss the lives and events of other people.

Self-taught millionaires talk about ideas. They have a vision, learn from each other, combine their strengths, and encourage each other in difficult times.

The poor will stay poor. And you around them too.

4. Think in numbers.

You must plan well. This means setting strict deadlines for each of your goals - knowing how much money to earn on what date.

Also, I know how much your time is worth. Don't underestimate it. In this way, you protect it more and ensure that you spend it in the most useful way.

Follow everything. Then go back to the results and analyze them. See what works well and save it. But do something for the rest.

5. Find what you are good at and manage it.

Speaking of making things, it works best when it comes to a skill that you already naturally possess and that you love. It is your so-called passion.

Everyone is good at something. Do some testing before you find that thing you can do for hours without getting bored.

Whatever the case, make sure you can turn it into a career and find a way to make money.

Passive Income Business Models

This chapter will define a passive income business model and present four popular, online passive business structures to the reader.

Developing a passive income business - What is a residual income model?

A residual or passive income asset is described as an economic flow of earnings, that upon a successful, initial setup, can guide its owner with a long-term influx of cash. This model of operation does no longer requires an active approach from the business owner and thus generates an inactive income.

The pros/cons of this business plan include:

- Able to generate a consistent stream of funds
- It does not require an active approach after initial setup (leaving the entrepreneur with more time on his hands)
- In comparison to an active stream of income, a passive one does not require heavy maintenance, diminishing the expenses of the business owner. Initial successful set-up is oftentimes hard to execute.

The residual income model has gained a solid online foundation, with the internet presenting ever more opportunities to its user-base. An online residual income stream holds many advantages, such as the simplification of the original set-up process, overall inexpensiveness, and the speediness of the set-up, over non-active income streams of the past.

Four of the most popular online passive income business models are:

- Affiliate marketing
- Information trade
- Selling information products
- Selling advertising space

The first of the four is the most popular choice of many entrepreneurs. Affiliate marketing is closely associated with multi-level marketing, yet it is quite different in many regards. Both of them amount to referring new clients and finding new sales leads for the service or product that is being promoted. However, affiliate marketing programs offer real services and products that solve needs and can benefit the consumer. MLM networks, on the other hand, are not stable passive income business models, as the product or service promoted within them is not the primary vehicle behind a sale. Thus no new wealth is generated.

Affiliate marketing means that we collaborate with a product or service provider and then set up a promotional campaign to bring the product to the attention of the masses. The affiliate marketer gets paid on a commission basis. A successfully executed promotional campaign is then able to generate residual income for the affiliate.

Another popular passive income business model lies in the trade of information. Here several instruction-type resources are set up by the entrepreneur; these receive an ongoing royalty-based commission or can be of promotional manner, thus binding in the previously mentioned business model. This type of passive income business model is attractive because of its simple initiation. It is, however, not the most efficient way to generate residual income, despite its non-complicated nature. Article marketing (as it falls under this type of business model), for example, can be very "slow-moving," and it might take up to 4 months to see some profits.

The next passive income business model is the most effective of the four but is also characterized by the most difficult initial set-up. The typical Internet user is a very "information-hungry" entity. Selling information products can be very lucrative if an entrepreneur is able to provide a unique, sought after solution or upgrade an already existing one. This business model requires an extensive knowledge base, as well as a good grasp of Internet marketing and product creation. Not to be attended by beginners.

The last passive income business model becomes feasible in combination with an already established, accessible Internet resource. This a source of non-active income if a blog or website generates a healthy amount of traffic. A popular niche blog, for example, can successfully sell advertisement space for about 1k-2k a month.

How To Make Money With A Business Model

Earning money while sleeping or traveling the world may seem like a dream to many people, but it is one of those dreams that can come true thanks to the power of web transformation.

To earn passive income, all you have to do is set up a system that allows you to sell products without having to work to make and deliver these products. This may mean that you are selling a digital product, such as an eBook, or selling a product on behalf of another company that acts as an affiliate. It may even mean that you earn money with advertisements.

And there are surprisingly some ways to proceed. Read on to know some of the best strategies you can use to generate passive income and how they work.

Sell an eBook from a sales page.

To create an eBook, simply choose a topic and write about it in a Word document. You can then save this document as a PDF file and start selling from your website. If you do not have the writing skills, knowledge, or patience to write an ebook, you can easily outsource this process by hiring an editor on a site like Fiverr, Elance, or UpWork.

Add an automated sales and distribution system, create an advertising campaign or an evergreen website, and you're ready to go!

Sell a Kindle eBook.

You can also simplify the sales process of eBooks via Kindle. Kindle is, of course, the name of the electronic reading device from Amazon, which also has its store books where users can find and download them. This makes it a very efficient distribution platform, which means that it is a straightforward way for you to find customers, sell them, and deliver your product. You do not have to worry about marketing, payment processing, or product delivery. Amazon does all this for you!

Surprising, it's free to sign up!

Sell an application

Or why not earn money with an app? It works as if you are selling a Kindle book because you have access to a ready-made distribution platform with a large audience. And if you promote your app on Android, you only need to pay $

30 to join up, and your app can be routinely approved inside hours.

Run a Website

Provided you can get enough visitors to a website, you can use it to make your ads profitable. Use AdSense, and every time a visitor clicks on an ad, you receive a minimal payment (usually a few cents per dollar). The most challenging thing is to get enough visitors to your site without having to spend every moment managing it. If you create an evergreen resource, or if you hire writers, it can work well.

Differences between Traditional Business and Passive Income Business

If you read the first two parts of this series, you've probably realized that not all businesses are passive income businesses. That's right, they are not, so let's dissect the two business models and see what the benefits are of a passive income business compared to a traditional business model.

How To Create Wealth: Traditional Business Drawbacks

The traditional business model has some benefits. However, it also has some severe defects, which will ultimately limit the overall wealth potential and passive income that the business owner can generate. The main benefit that is owning a business provides is that of leverage.

Leverage is the ability to use other peoples' time, knowledge, and skills to generate results that you otherwise would not or could not alone. For example, if I chose to work 24 hours a day for five days, I could only work a total of 120 hours. However, if I employed 200 workers and only asked them to work one hour a day for five days, they would have accomplished 1,000 total hours-worth of work. That is the power of leverage.

There are many drawbacks to consider, as well. Aside from overhead expenses from rent, insurance, legal work, the main problem is derived from the hiring of employees. Yes, these employees provide you the leverage to accomplish more than you could alone, but that might not be good enough. Non-performance based employees have no real incentive to assist the owners in growing the business.

Excluding a sales or trading position where the performance can be tracked, and they can be paid a percentage of their performance, it becomes very difficult to pay other employees based on performance. This leads to an issue where the employees generally only work as much as needed not to lose their jobs, and the employer pays them just as much as needed to make sure they don't leave. It stumps the full potential of growth for the employees and the company overall.

How To Create Wealth: Network Marketing Benefits

Network Marketing is an optimal passive or residual income business, which is just now being realized for its full potential. There's a lot of misconception about the industry; however, it is a great business model that allowed the top 7 publicly traded Network Marketing companies to average a 268% increase in stock price from March 2009 to May 2011. That was a period that many other industries were doing much worse.

It's such a beautiful industry in that by helping other people become successful; you can attain your success. It's an industry where the average person can choose to learn and work hard to create an above-average income and lifestyle. There are many benefits to a Network Marketing Business, which has probably led to the massive growth over the last few years, while other industries are struggling.

Network Marketing Benefits

- Unlimited Earning Potential
- Leverage Multiplied
- Tax Advantages (Home-Based Business)
- Work From Home (or Remotely)
- No Overhead Expenses (Rent, Insurance, etc.)
- Legal work is handled for you
- Accounting is handled for you
- Production and distribution of products/services is handled for you

The Network Marketing model allows the individual to focus solely on product or service distribution and to grow the distribution or network with other like-minded people. The industry is completely performance-based. Therefore it is in everyone's best interest to work as best they can because if they don't, they are directly hurting their own potential for success.

Leverage multiplied comes from the concept that not only are you able to leverage the efforts of other distributors you introduce into the network, but you will support them to the best of your ability to succeed. Your success is based upon their success and vice versa. They will work to the best of their abilities for you and the company because their earning potential is performance-based. You will do your best to support and guide them to success, as they will provide you success since they are within your network. You are both leveraging each other, but within that, the whole network is leveraging each other, so you have a massive support structure in place that all benefits by helping others.

Where can you find great resources online for your passive income company?

Building a passive online business does not require plenty of effort in case you know what to do. The net has nearly the whole thing you want to develop your source of income. There are forums, blogs, and web sites for beginners that assist you to with primary guidelines and guide you. If you may prepare the blueprint, you're only a step behind the fulfillment - enforcing the thoughts. Here, you may discover some locations in which you can locate resourceful data approximately building your passive profits generator online.

Places where you can find beneficial assets for constructing a passive income business

Several websites will help you recognize the concept of passive earnings generators online. You want to comply with the publications and have a well-known idea about that first! Earlier than you flow on, you may need to understand how the system works, and right here, you may find about some outstanding locations wherein you should hold out earlier than you jump into a passive commercial enterprise online.

Social websites

In recent times, social websites are getting extremely popular as assets for brand new marketers willing to set up an enterprise online. Facebook, Twitter, and different main web sites have plenty of businesses and pages wherein you can discover ingenious information. At the equal time, you'll be in a position to hook up with the market leaders and analyze new stuff. These social profiles may even assist you in digging useful facts without tons of search on the internet.

Forum

There are loads of boards online in which enthusiastic marketers are engaged in different discussions. Digital factor, Warrior discussion board, Site point, etc., are some of the exceptional locations to hang out for the brand new marketers round. These forums include big facts, associated data and adventure revel in, and so forth. You just need to open an account, get worried, and start studying from scratch. If you're a novice, you'll want to apprehend a suitable business version and start operating on it.

Webinars

Webinars are one of the excellent sources where you may learn about a passive business model extra exactly. You want to preserve your eyes huge open and discover the associated webinars to wait. Some of these are free to participate in, while you have to pay a nominal rate to attend.

Blogs

Following the blogs also can be very useful. Nearly all leading entrepreneurs have their blogs in which they proportion their views and enjoy approximately distinct sorts of stuff. You need to subscribe to their blogs or bookmark them. Following those blogs will assist you in experiencing the journey and research new stuff.

A Way to Convert Any commercial enterprise model into a Passive Income Generator?

Passive income generator refers to a commercial enterprise model that can run on autopilot or that has less supervision.

All business models may be transformed into passive profits generator. And a good passive income generator will help you to establish a reliable cash flow and a supplement to your finances. Here, in this part, you will discover the secrets of converting a business into a safe, long-term passive revenue generator. Let's find out some fantastic tips from successful business entrepreneurs and learn how they established some of the best successful passive income businesses ever.

Converting a regular business model into a passive income generator: some tips from the successful entrepreneurs

Some of the most successful entrepreneurs have come up with their special tips and suggestions, and those are discussed here. You can follow these strategies and can automate the model to a greater extent. Your efforts will optimize the system and establish an automated system that works in real.

Creating a strong customer base:

If you have a vast customer base, you don't have to concentrate on marketing and sales anymore. You have to retain the customers and entertain them with high quality, dedicated services. As an example, if you have prepared software, you have to promote the software in the beginning. Later, all you need to do is retaining the customers and enhancing the quality of services your software is offering.

Automate the operation

If you've already established a business, and it has a strong customer base, you have to focus on automating the operation. You have to divide the operation into a few departments and distribute the operational duties and responsibilities. You can also hire a supervisor or a manager to take care of the operation in your absence. If you have an online business, choose a combination of the latest technologies to automate the operation more efficiently.

Offer franchising opportunities

Nowadays, the maximum hit enterprise models offer franchising possibilities. If you have developed a new brand and want to expand the business automatically, start offering franchise opportunities. You have to prepare a good, convincing business proposal and tell the interested partners about the benefits of the franchise opportunity. If you're good at selling, you'll be able to get lots of offers to finance your business and yourself in an autopilot process.

Develop a brand to generate clients and business deals

The most important and effective method to convert a business model into a passive revenue cash flow is to develop a brand name. A reliable brand doesn't need active promotions. And a reliable brand always has an autopilot system that works all together. So you should concentrate on developing brands than anything. Once you have established a business and attained the brand-fame, you're just about to develop the most reliable passive income business model.

Chapter summary

There are several ways to develop a money-making non-active income source. It is crucial to start with the most straightforward option available, get your feet wet, and then proceed to more advanced passive income business models. Try to gain as much information as possible, either through Google or an educational resource of your choice, in order to avoid the possibility of costly mistakes.

Chapter 3

Assets and Liabilities

If you want to become rich and want to retire earlier, the most important thing you will learn is the difference between an asset and a liability. Wealthy people understand the difference and buy assets that enrich them; the poor and the middle class don't understand the difference and therefore make poor investment decisions that only make them worse instead of enriching.

People work their entire lives to get more productive, but with every salary, their debt increases, as does their spending. This increase in debts and expenses forces them to work harder to make ends meet. With a simple understanding of the difference between assets and liabilities, these people can become more productive and richer instead of becoming poorer and poorer.

If you go to your bank and ask them what an asset is, they will tell you that everything you own has a monetary value.

But this is often inflated because the value is only an idea until it is actually sold. That is not a plus. Your costumes, your computer, your PlayStation, your cars are not assets but liabilities. You have to start thinking if you want to become rich when the rich and the rich think differently about assets and liabilities.

Simplifying the concept of an asset is something that regularly puts money in your pocket, and an obligation is something that periodically costs you money. For example, your car is not a plus; it is an obligation because you can use it to take money for gas, insurance, registration, and maintenance. Your house where you live is not a plus but an obligation because it allows you to collect money for maintenance work, insurance, municipal taxes, etc., in your pocket on a regular basis or take money.

An asset, therefore, puts money in your pocket and a money obligation. Wealthy people know the difference between assets and liabilities and buy assets. By purchasing assets that generate income, you increase your resources. If you continue to use your money wisely, your income will gradually increase, and it will become easier to get richer.

Lots of people will tell you that it is smart to save money. But the rich think that saving money is risky. The cost of living is rising steadily due to inflation, which means that the purchasing power of the dollar declines every year. My mother used to buy a candy bag for a penny when she was a child, and now you can hardly buy a candy bag for $1. It's the same, but the purchasing power of the dollar has declined. For example, the value of your money decreases every year when you save it.

However, if you buy an asset such as an investment property and the purchasing power of the dollar decreases, the price of your property for compensation increases; not only that, but your rents also increase to compensate. All inflation-related expenses are passed on to other people, so you don't lose any money at all. If you save money in the bank, $100,000 is worth much less in 10 years today.

The rich do not work for money but to buy assets that generate income for them. They understand that money is falling in value, and they want to purchase assets that suit them, so they don't have to work for money. The two rich people are poor people who go to work, but their motives provide bipolar results. We become richer as they work less and less and become more miserable as they work more and more.

Assets and Liabilities: The Key to Wealth

Assets and Liabilities are two terms that I am sure that you have heard before. They are usually associated with the balance sheet. On the balance sheet, assets are what you own, and liabilities are what you owe to others. In determining your net worth or the net worth of your company, you would subtract the value of your liabilities from the value of your assets. The number that you come up with is what is called your net worth.

Defining Assets

The financial benefit of everything the organization owns is called the asset. Put, resources are the questions that can be converted into money as quickly as possible or can generate a salary for the organization. This is useful for paying a commitment or the cost of the substance. Accounting divides resources into two general classes as follows:

- Fixed assets
- Long term investments

- Tangible fixed assets
- Intangible assets

Current assets

In cash

Debtor

investments

inventory

Costs paid upfront

Define Liabilities

The financial estimate of an obligation or commitment of the organization towards another person or association is called risk. In simple terms, the obligation consists of debt arising from previous grants, which must be paid by the organization as quickly as possible, thanks to the benefits of the element. Accounting divides liabilities into two general categories that are:

- Long-term liability
- Long-term loans
- bonds

Current liabilities

Account due

Short-term loan

Unpaid costs

Bank credit

The accounting recipe is the way double accounting is built. The accounting recipe, also called a mathematical overview of currency registration, talks about the relationship between the benefits, obligations, and the value of a small business by the owner. It is important to understand the accounting comparison to understand how you can view an asset report. Similarly, it is important to understand the accounting recipe to understand the relationship between the money statements of the organization.

Relationship Between Assets and Liabilities:

The accounting income essentially shows what the company claims (its benefits) are purchased by what it owes (its obligations) or by what its owners bring (value for its shareholders or capital). This relationship is communicated in the form of a mathematical explanation:

Assets = liabilities + equity

This mathematical statement must be adjusted because everything that the company owns (resources) must be acquired with something, either a risk or the capital of the owner. Resources refer to items such as shares or receivables.

Active and passive - Knowing the difference can mean anything!

Whether you are an accounting officer or not, everyone needs to understand the facts about assets and liabilities. Understanding the difference between them can mean the difference between becoming rich or becoming poor. The purpose of this chapter is to explain the difference between these two accounts and to provide basic accounting knowledge that even the weakest person can learn to understand finances.

Assets are whatever that may be owned with the aid of a man or woman or a company that has a positive cash value. In other words, assets generate income. What are some examples of assets? Investments, real estate, companies are all examples of things that can save you more money than you originally invested. Assets are things on which you can see an ROI (Return on Investment). Assets can be classified into three categories. There are current assets, tangible fixed assets, and intangible assets. Understanding the difference between these three classifications can be very useful to decipher how income is recorded in the financial statements.

Current assets are considered as cash or assets that can be converted to cash in a short period of time. Current assets finance daily activities. Companies use short-term assets to manage their daily activities because it is better to spend money on short-term financing. Five different accounts are listed under current assets. These accounts include cash, investments, debtors, inventories, and prepaid expenses.

Tangible assets are considered as material ownership. Fixed assets require time to be converted into cash as current assets. Capital assets include real estate, machinery and equipment, and buildings. There are other items, such as computers, that can be considered as fixed assets. It is, therefore, best to contact an accountant to find out what can be considered as fixed assets. Capital assets are subject to special tax treatment and can also be written off.

Intangible assets are considered to be monetary items that cannot be physically affected. These items can be converted to cash but generally retain value for the individual or business entity. Examples of intangible assets are patents, trademarks, and copyrights. There are two types of intangible assets, classified as legal intangible and competitive intangible assets. It is recommended to consult your accountant for more advice on intangible assets.

Now that we have covered the assets, we have to talk about the "double obligations." Liability is everything that is owned by an individual or company and must be repaid. Obligations do not generate money but cost us money. Liabilities are debts that have to be repaid and normally with interest. There are two classifications in which obligations can be classified. There are short-term debts and long-term debts. These two categories of obligations must be repaid and are considered as debts.

Current liabilities are considered as a debt that must be repaid within one year. This debt is usually repaid via the current account; however, this is not always the case. There are many categories of current liabilities. Some categories of short-term debts are payable bonds, bills to be paid, short-term debts, and dividends to be paid.

Long-term debts or obligations are regarded as debts that can be repaid after one year. An example of long-term debts would be a lease or deferred taxes.

After explaining the differences between what is considered an asset and what is considered a liability, it's clear that it is in the interest of the individual and the company to have much more assets than liabilities. This is how people get rich because they try not to get too many obligations, especially if income-generating assets cannot pay them.

Chapter 4

Secrets to Repairing Bad Credit Score

We have talked a lot about good and bad credit assessments lately. It is no secret that many people realize that their ratings are stopping them. Bad credit prevents them from owning a house, going to school, or even buying a car. So what is a bad credit score? The conditions have changed a little over the past decade. What was considered good was reduced to the right category, making it much more difficult to obtain preferential interest rates on loans.

Following are five things you should consider about scores and how you can determine what bad credit is compared to a good score.

- A poor score is truly subjective, relying on the credit implemented for. Domestic loans have a number of the strictest credit standards, even as department save credit playing cards have fantastically lax standards. Housing loans are typical of the opinion that below

640 is an awful figure; however, that doesn't necessarily imply which you can't get a housing mortgage for some applications.

- Credit card companies often offer credit lines to people with a score between 500 and 600, but the interest rates are lower than the prime rate. Additional costs can also be added.
- If it is a bad score, it is important to understand that scores below 500 are considered very bad. People with such low scores will have trouble getting unsecured loans or lines of credit. However, it is not the end of the world. It is possible to increase a credit score.
- Unfortunately, not much is needed to drop a credit score. Late payment, bankruptcy, or a medical bill sent as recovery can reduce the score by two digits. In fact, it takes very little time, a few months, before a score is negatively affected, but the repair can take months or even years.
- Consumers whose scores are in the poor credit range pay almost double the interest compared to those with scores above 640. It is very expensive to get a car loan with an interest rate of essentially punitive interests. Many consumers are better off saving money at a

bank and buying what they need instead of getting a high-interest loan.

Understanding the impact of scores on interest rates on loans and credit cards is an important step in rebuilding credit. Before he asks for credit, the consumer must understand what a bad credit score is. Never assume that a score is good or bad before you know the facts. Choose wisely when it comes to applying for new credit. Do not be fooled by the high-interest rates that cost you more money and make you more indebted, which damages your credit score further than it already is.

Fixing Bad Credit Scores

When you hear a credit repair company talking about "fixing credit scores," you may start wondering how they do it. Are there any special tricks? Does it even work? Is it a scam? It's never a bad idea to question these companies. After all, your time and money are on the line.

So what's the Secret to Fixing Bad Credit Scores?

There's no secret. In fact, improving your score can be pretty straightforward and simple. It takes a little time and a little dedication. So if you're ready to start making changes, here are simple five ways that you can improve your score.

1. Make sure your report is accurate - this is normally one of the first steps in the repair process. Ensuring that there are no mistakes on your report is important-even minor mistakes can have a negative impact on your score.
2. Lower your credit card balances - the more debt you're in, the more of a risk you appear to be to lenders. Avoid this by paying down your credit card balances, and staying within 10% of your credit limit may be ideal.
3. Establish new lines of credit - this may not apply to everyone, but if you don't have a sufficient credit history, you may want to consider getting new lines of credit. The often-recommended number of cards to have is 3. If you don't have at least a couple, maybe adding an addition to your profile will help raise your score.
4. Make your payments on time - many people fail to realize how much late payments can hurt your credit score. And many are in the regular habit of paying late. Start being on time! There's nothing a creditor

loves to see more than prompt payment history, so stay on top of things and make sure you pay your bills on time every month.

5. Age your credit - by aging your credit, you are not only managing it responsibly and paying your bills on time, but you are showing lenders that you've got what it takes to make a good thing last. And that's what they like to see. So hold onto your credit and maintain it. The longer you show that you're capable of having credit, the better your credit will be.

There's no guarantee that every credit repair company can get you the results you want. But by understanding how credit repair works, you'll be able to spot the companies that just don't offer the services you need. Look for a company that takes these five steps to fix bad credit scores. If they don't, keep looking-they won't be able to take you very far.

The best way to begin correcting a bad credit rating is to practice credit-building behavior, like paying bills on time. Your credit score will improve every month as you continue making monthly payments on time. It also improves by repaying past due amounts and cleaning up collection accounts.

Remember to consider this when seeking to hire a credit repair company: Companies that can help you re-establish your credit will charge a fee, but that fee should not be charged until the work is completed. Although it's not necessary to pay a third party to help repair bad credit, it can definitely help.

Credit bureaus do not remove accurate information from your credit report. The only way to get negative information removed is to rectify the debt properly. Only incorrect info can be deleted from your credit report. There are no secret tricks or loopholes that credit repair companies exclusively know to get correct information off your credit report. Their help can be beneficial because they are more familiar with the process but know this: No credit repair company is able to do anything you can't do for yourself. It is impossible for anyone or any agency to make changes in your file if the facts have been correctly reported.

Chapter 5

How to be Profitable

The purpose that all and sundry go into business is to make a profit, simple, and simple. Many commercial enterprise owners emerge as spending an entire lot of time analyzing income figures and assuming that they may, by some means, make an income. Sadly, however, many enterprise proprietors do no longer see what they are doing incorrectly till the quit of the business 12 months, while it's far often too late.

If you are a business owner and want to know how to increase profit all year long, it takes a bit of imagination and knowledge, but once you receive some tips, you should be well on your way to turning the numbers favorably in your direction.

One of the best ways to increase your profits is to take a look at how you market your products or services. If you are spending a huge deal of money advertising but not seeing whether or not this investment is paying off, you could be throwing money out the window. You should keep a close eye on where your sales are coming from. You can obtain this information by asking your customers how they found you. If you discover that the advertisements you place in the local newspapers are not what is attracting people to your business, then you would benefit from discontinuing this form of advertisement and putting that money into something that is actually attracting customers.

Another rather obvious way of how to increase profit is to raise the prices of your products or services. Many business owners are hesitant to take this step for fear that that competitor will steal their share of the market. However, if you use clever marketing techniques that make your products seem superior to your competitor's, consumers will be much more willing to pay a bit extra. If you are hesitant to raise all of your prices, simply conduct a small sample test by raising the prices of just a few of your products to test the waters. Leave the higher prices in effect for at least two months so that you can clearly see if sales drop, remain the same, or actually climb.

Keep an eye on your expenses. If possible, limit your travels and instead make use of the latest technologies such as webinars and conference calls. Sometimes a simple phone call is enough to seal a deal as opposed to setting aside several hours to meet with a prospective customer in person. If you are spending a good deal of money on office supplies such as copy paper, ink, etc., find ways to cut the usage of these items, as very often businesses waste a lot of money and resources printing off material that is not ever read or used. Keep an eye on your utility costs in your place of business as well. Turn the thermostat down, shut off lights in rooms not being used, and look into changing your utility company so that you can save money.

These tips, when implemented, should help your company increase profits. You have undoubtedly invested a good deal of both your time and money into your business with the hopes of making a turning a respectable profit. Cutting a few expenditures, raising prices, and seeing how you are spending your advertising money are sure-fire ways of succeeding.

Tips To Increase Profits In Your Business

While there is no magic way to generate money and make a profit, there are things you can do to improve your financial growth on a regular basis.

A widespread rule for your monetary success in business is which you can't boom income directly but in a roundabout way. You cannot simply say that you are increasing the profit of your business without a specific strategy.

The major thing you can do to increase your profit is to improve the variables that ultimately determine your profitability. When you improve these ten variables for your business, you increase your profit and influence your business results.

1) Lead generation

The process that you use to attract potential customers who are interested in your business. If five out of ten potential customers who come to your company end up buying from you and you'll be able to increase some of the people in a range of 10 to 15, you can earn more money and increase your earnings by 50%.

2) Lead conversion

The process by which you convert potential customers into paying customers. That is the degree of the effectiveness of your income efforts. If you could grow your conversion charge from one in ten to 2 in ten, you can double your sales and raise up your profit.

One of the most significant things you can do is improve your sales capacity and turn your interested prospects into paying customers. And nothing can replace the ongoing sales training, both for you and for every person who talks to customers, live or over the phone.

View all the important result areas of your sales process and look for ways to improve a little in each area. A small improvement in every important area can lead to a significant improvement in overall sales results.

By applying continuous improvement to all of these areas of your business, you will earn more money, increase your company profits, and contribute to your future financial success!

With sufficient insight and planning, you can make a profit in your company and make it negotiable. Tony Robbins is the world's number 1 strategist in life and business and has launched several successful companies whether you are in search of ways to increase the profit of your business or want to know more about how you can remove the limiting beliefs in business.

Chapter 6

Dropshipping Made Easy

Dropshipping has become a well-known online business idea because it's simple to set up, needs little investment, and the market is huge.

What is dropshipping?

Dropshipping is an online company in which an online store does not keep products in stock, which means that there are no inventory costs. Instead, as soon as the customer buys a product, the shop owner places an order with the initial vendor and delivers the item directly to the customer.

The drop shipping business model has some advantages and disadvantages that you must take into account before you start.

Advantages of starting a dropshipping store

- Setting up a dropshipping company requires a much lower investment than a classical online store.
- You don't have to buy products or manage inventory
- You do not have to ship the product yourself
- You can sell a variety of products from different sellers and manufacturers

Disadvantages of starting a dropshipping store

- It can be hard to manage customer expectations if you have no control over the quality or shipment of products.
- Customer support may be hard.
- You're going to create less profit because instead of purchasing wholesale products, you're only selling one product at a time.

Before deciding on a Dropship option that is suitable for you, list the following:

- ➢ Product(s) you are planning to dropship.
- ➢ The amount you could spend.
- ➢ Do you prefer to try the service before buying it?
- ➢ Are you planning to sell your products on eBay?

Most of the dropship services charge you a monthly fee or upfront one-off payment to use their services. If you're a beginner to dropshipping, you could try a dropship service like Doba, which offers a 7-day trial. This would be enough time to find out whether the drop-off service is appropriate for you. Your choice should be based on the accessibility of the item you are planning to drop and the vendors you have access to. Another benefit is that Doba is licensed by eBay, meaning that you can dropship products accessible through Doba on eBay.

SaleHoo is another great drop ship service if you're new to drop. Not only do they ensure you a provider, but they also provide a 60-day money-back guarantee if you're not pleased with it. This would be a reasonable time to figure out whether or not your business model will work for you.

Dropshipping is an outstanding way to begin an internet retail business with little investment. The products you choose to drop are critical to the profitability of your company.

Everyone in the world has seen a world of change in recent decades. One of the newest online business ideas is about shuttle services. This online business involves a process whereby manufacturers or suppliers deliver the products directly to the customers of the drop-load company without having to buy from the company. Advance or store the goods.

The owner of the direct transportation service company only needs to list the products on eBay and receive orders for those products using his descriptions and charts, as well as those of the company. When orders are obtained, the reseller shall provide data on the names and addresses of the purchasers, as well as other details of the order, so that the vendor may send the goods to the purchaser. The business shall also receive the payment.

The dropship service company can pay a lot to the owner, but the leading dropshipping guide is that it is necessary to take care of the business and customers to ensure that the buyers' claims regarding the poor quality of the product or delays received between payments. And the delivery of goods tends to be fast.

Steps to successfully start a Dropship company

The explosion of the internet in the past two decades has created unprecedented opportunities for home use. The auction giant eBay has gone from an idea to a billion dollars with millions of dollars in different hands every day. Many people have become "energy sellers" on eBay and have created great home businesses by listing and selling items on eBay. While everyone hears stories about who finds a rare diamond or antique baseball card in an old dresser, there are many more sellers who have created legitimate businesses using a shuttle model to buy and sell goods.

Using a direct selling method online is a great way to sell products because you never have to have an item to sell for profit physically. The function of dropshipping is that you find an item from a company or manufacturer at a certain price, sell it online for a higher price, and the company where you buy the product delivers the product.\ It is a "winner" for you and the company that you are going through because it sells an item and makes a profit, and you do it yourself.

Many "virtual" shops that often resemble big warehouses are merely individuals who send goods from the comfort of their homes to clients. If you're interested in beginning your dropship company, here are some things you might need to do before you begin your company.

Five steps to successfully start a Dropship company

Establish a business: research and establish a business entity that best meets your objectives. To establish a corporate identity, you must complete the correct forms in your state and pay a small fee before you begin. This will be your first step because many companies that offer drop shipping services will not work with "individuals," but only with companies.

Do market research: do market research on the items you want to sell and see what the online prices are for these items. When doing drop shipping, it is often best to stick with items that sell for more than $ 100 because smaller items offer little benefit to a dropship company. View important devices, televisions, and other items that you can expect to earn at least $ 25 or more for each sale.

Contact major manufacturers: for each store item that you want to sell, it is advisable to contact the services of the major companies that sell these items. Make sure you present yourself as a company when you call and ask if you can open a business account with their company. Also, make sure they give a decrease in shipping facilities because double shipping expenses are not worth your time and effort.

Develop an internet presence: the best way to begin is to set up an eBay account and list your products individually. Once you've discovered products that sell well or want to specialize, many individuals often build an online store through eBay or by establishing their own website.

Marketing of products: do extensive research on others who are successful online and follow their format. If you're having trouble writing ads or listing products, search for a seller page and use their ads as a guide to selling items. Also, participate in forums and talk to other people who have been successful with a home business or who are interested in becoming an entrepreneur.

With the spectacular growth of the internet, people become millionaires every day. One of these ways is to develop a profitable home business. Follow these steps and develop your own dropshipping company today.

How To Find, Analyze And Sell Physical Products For Your Own Dropshipping Business

When it comes to selling physical items online, I always like to begin with a set of rules during the product selection process.

Because selling online is completely different from selling in a physical store, you want to choose which products you want to sell that are beneficial for online shopping and are attractive to the typical online shopper.

Here are some of my "must-have" guidelines for choosing products for sale.

The product must not be fragile and easy to ship. Because we ship products by mail, you could avoid most headaches if you select a product to sell that does not break during shipping.

The product may not take up much physical space. Some e-commerce business models must keep an inventory. It is therefore in your interest to choose a small product that you can sell, preferably an item that slips into a shoebox.

The intrinsic value of the product must be ambiguous. For example, I would never sell electronic goods because there is a fixed value for your products that everyone knows. On the contrary, souvenirs and information goods are much harder to sell.

The product must be timeless - Again, I will never sell electronic products because they lose more value and stay on the shelves

Avoid seasonal products - In general, you do not want to opt for products that were only purchased during a certain period of the year.

Sell products that sell between 15 and 200 USD - This is the ideal starting point for prices for online shopping

The following product guidelines are "useful" when you choose what you want to sell so that you can ask yourself the following questions.

Have you selected a niche with related products in which you can grow? - Although we mainly sell tissues in our store, we have qualified our linen store, allowing us to expand into other markets easily.

Do your items lend themselves to clients who purchase a few? - When we sell handkerchiefs to a bride, we rarely sell just one. However, a typical bride buys at least four and sometimes at most ten.

Can you customize your products? – The margins for personalized goods will always be higher than for standard goods. So if you can offer custom products, you can pay more for them.

Are your products consumable? - The good thing about consumables is that your number of loyal customers will be high. As a result, your sales are generally more stable.

Does your niche have a fan base? - I like to choose products with blogs or special fan pages because you immediately have a number of customers on the market.

Are your products suitable for creating content? - When you have your own store, search engine optimization is an excellent source of traffic to your store. As a result, the more content you broadcast, the greater the chance that you will receive a rank.

Do you have a lot of accessories for your products? -Many online stores make up the bulk of their margin on the accessories they sell. It is, therefore, in your interest to offer products that lead to more sales and cross-selling.

Chapter 7

Getting Started With Listing And Launching Products On eBay And Amazon

Are you wondering how to locate products for sale on Amazon and eBay? Have you been trawling around eBay for hours looking for inspiration but can't decide what would be the best item to sell? Do you feel overwhelmed by information to the point where you don't know where to begin? You're not the only one.

Many people who are desperate to start their own online business have been reluctant for months, or even years, because they don't understand how to discover products to sell on eBay that will make every auction a success. It doesn't have to be that way! Finding the best items for the maximum profit can be as easy as 1, 2, 3.

1. What do you WANT to sell?

We're so caught up in worrying about how to find products to sell on eBay for profit that we forget to think about what we want to sell.

What do you like to buy? That might be an excellent starting point when it comes to thinking about what to sell. Pick something you're genuinely interested in! The belief that no one enjoys work can be broken if you're dealing with something that you love every day.

2. Is what you want to sell selling?

Hopefully, in deciding what you want to sell, you will have come up with a couple of potential ideas. To determine which is the best, you will have to spend a bit of time discovering whether said products will make you any money. Do individuals really want it? It's straightforward to figure out! Spend a few hours looking at some of the large online retailers like Amazon and see if your products are listed there. Have they got a lot of client feedback? If so, they're probably going to sell well. You could also look for forums and blogs that cover the region where you're selling essential hints about the real products that individuals are after. Just type 'your product' followed by the word 'forum' into Google to find out what's on people's minds.

3. Can you buy what you want to sell cheaply?

To make money, you need to sell products for a profit. That means buying cheaply and selling at a higher price. The greater the gap between the purchase cost and the selling price, the better! You'll need to consider where you can get your hands on some inventory when you think about how to find products to sell on eBay. There's plenty of options that might work for you; here's just a few:

Your garage, attic, or the back of the wardrobe -Charity stores -Car boot sales or flea markets - Online drop-shippers (give them order data, and they will post the item to the customer)-Wholesalers (they will sell their products to you at a discounted price).

The sky is the limit when it comes to the possibilities offered.

Use your imagination, be creative, and shortly you'll find the best item to sell to make real cash on eBay from now on!

How To Source Products To Sell On eBay

It doesn't matter whether you're a technical specialist or a beginner in electricity. It doesn't matter if you put a whizz kid on the market or if you've never sold your life. eBay can provide you with a part or full-time revenue wherever you are... If you are considering earning extra money this way, you may be wondering why more people are not benefiting from it, especially if it is that easy.

Unfortunately, all of this is usually due to a poor selection of products that are for sale on eBay. Without the right product to sell, it becomes harder to earn a living with our favorite internet auction website. Fortunately, however, you have come across a tool that you need to point in the right direction to find quality products that can be purchased at great profit.

Insight into the market

It makes no sense to buy a product on which you can sell if you cannot make a profit for your efforts. Understanding the market is a key step in learning how to make money on eBay because this market knowledge gives you all the information you need to know the items that potential buyers are looking for.

Market research is not something that requires practice. That's why you need to know how to search for industries that you're interested in to assist you find products for sale on eBay. Why not spend some time looking around eBay now, as well as other large retail stores such as Amazon, to give you an idea of some of the products that are selling successfully today.

Understanding the Product

I hope your market research has given you some ideas for potential products that can be successfully sold on eBay. Scroll through your list and determine what you know about each of these topics. In the beginning, it may not seem that important, but buying and selling products you are familiar with will help you in many ways. On the one hand, you know how to find deals that help you sell merchandise for big profits. On the other hand, thanks to your expertise in the field, you can write incredible descriptions that encourage buyers to buy from you.

Insight into the sources

Of course, it is not useful to have an idea of the ideal product to sell if you really cannot get it. There are different options when it comes to searching for products to sell on eBay.

Many of these options are viable, but some outperform others if you plan to use eBay as a source of full-time income. Here are some examples that you can view to get you started:

- Charity shops/sales of car boots
- wholesalers
- Dropshippers
- Liquidation of street shops
- Products sold under their value on eBay itself

Search for products offered for sale with Amazon sales data

Amazon is slowly becoming the de facto standard for internet shopping in the United States, with the largest internet market share of any business.

As a result, Amazon's derived sales data is an excellent representation of total demand. More and more people go directly to Amazon for ALL their online shopping needs while avoiding Google and the small online stores.

At first glance, it is not clear that you can get real sales figures from Amazon; below is how you can proceed.

Note: every item sold on Amazon receives a BSR: Best Selling Rank?

Amazon uses this figure to rate the sales level of a product relative to others in the same category.

So what does the BSR say about a particular product? Based on the BSR, you can accurately guess the number of units sold per day.

In short, you can consult Amazon for product ideas and know-how well a product sells by consulting BSR. And through perseverance and hard work, you can probably find a profitable niche to pursue.

How To Find Products To Sell Using eBay Sales Data

Like Amazon, eBay is also a great place to search for potential products that can be purchased in your online store. Although Amazon is a much bigger market, eBay is a beautiful place to explore because you have access to real-time sales information.

Many bulk goods from Asia are sold at a low cost on eBay and listed on eBay for profit. However, as Ebay's selling expenses are quite high, it is hard to create a nice profit at the auctions.

So if you can find the much-needed products on eBay and create an online store for these items, you may be able to make a lot of sales, and you don't have to pay heavy expenses.

My wife and I began on eBay with a list of our auction goods so that we could assess the demand before we introduced our complete online store!

If you want to think about products for sale on eBay, type an item in the eBay search bar.

- Search eBay
- Then look for the "Sold items" link in the sidebar and select the checkbox.

eBay now displays a list of products sold in the product category of your choice, as well as the final selling price. With this information, you should be able to get a good idea of the demand and the selling price of a wide range of products.

Now, using the above method to evaluate the application works well, but it is incredibly annoying, so I like to use the Terapeak tool for easier searching.

Terapeak is a tool that retrieves all eBay lists and collects data for you in an organized way.

For example, with just a few mouse clicks, Terapeak can tell me which products are the most popular on eBay and how much it generated revenue last month.

More importantly, Terapeak informs me how exactly the proportion of offers for a particular item resulted in a sale with crucial information on the demand for a product.

Listing on Each Site

The listing process is very different between Amazon and eBay because Amazon has product pages already defined; all you have to do is tell Amazon that you have the item, how many you have, and what your price is. A few clicks and you are done.

eBay is more work because each product that you sell has its product page that has to be created. That means typing out titles, taking and uploading pictures, writing descriptions, and setting all of your seller-specific settings on the eBay listing page.

What Items Sell Best on Each Site

Amazon and eBay are both great sites for selling stuff, but certain items certainly do better on each site.

Amazon is great for new items, commodity-type items, and items of which you have multiple,

identical quantities. You can sell practically anything on Amazon, and if it already has a product page, you can have your items offered for sale in a matter of seconds; just find the product page for the item, enter the quantity that you have for sale, enter your price, and you're done. If it isn't on Amazon, you can choose to build a fresh product page. This is not difficult and normally requires a UPC on the product.

It is more work than listing on an existing product page, but the good news is that you only have to create the product page one time. Creating new product pages can be very rewarding, as you can enjoy being the exclusive seller on Amazon.

eBay is great for items that may not have product pages on Amazon. eBay is also great for one-of-a-kind items as well as collectible items. Many collectors will always check eBay for those specific, hard-to-find items that may not get listed anywhere else.

Many items will sell well on both sites. An eBay buyer's money is not worth less than an Amazon buyer's money, so don't turn away buyers or sales for no reason. Some buyers go to eBay first out of preference or out of habit. They may still believe that Amazon only sells books.

Launch Products Online to Increase Your Dollars

If you have to choose one thing that is most crucial for the achievement of a fresh product, it has to be the product launch. Irrespective of the type of item you market, its implementation will immediately determine the success or failure of this product. Some research has been done into product marketing to generate maximum profit in the introductory phase.

Launching a product needs a lot of planning in terms of client focus, sales, distribution, training, and growth of the sales department, and so on... It's not just about bringing a product from your production plant to the market, but you can also do it so that the product is visible and available to the right people, in the right direction, and at the right time.

Before companies launch a new product, they must do a lot of basic research. They must identify the best customer segments and the best positioning strategy in relation to the competition. Distribution channels and their management also play a crucial part in the achievement of a product, as they must be accessible to the correct individuals who are your target market segment. It is also very important for the company to identify the best marketing mix for the new product, including price, distribution, packaging, and product features.

Today, a lot of things have altered because of the refinement of clients and technology. Companies must have an integrated attitude to the launch of fresh products. This integration needs businesses to simultaneously develop and execute traditional internet and social marketing instruments for the launch of their products.

Products are exposed to the masses through traditional methods such as television, radio, and print media. Because these traditional methods are still attractive, they are usually used for new product launches in the retail and manufacturing sectors. Also, to these methods, the importance of fairs, promotional events, direct mail, advertisements, etc., cannot be ignored. These are proven methods that will certainly attract the consumer's attention.

Email campaigns have proven to be very useful in building a brand for the launch of a new product. Online advertising, through popular channels, such as pay-per-click service or Google AdWords, also has an important effect on client purchase behavior.

In the era of social networking, it would be dumb to ignore social applications like Twitter, Facebook, and Instagram.

These websites are extremely popular with people of all ages and backgrounds. This allows you to expose yourself to a wide audience, young and old.

Blogs, on the other hand, have also found their way to product launches due to their growing attraction to the masses. Similarly, selling online is another excellent way to influence the successful introduction of a product. If you can't open your own online store configuration, you can collaborate with big names such as Amazon, Google Product Search, eBay, and more.

Many forms of advertising can be used to launch a product. When you launch a new product, you must have some marketing experience or be a partner with an experienced person or company. Product launches are significant and enable companies to save energy online and offline.

Launch a product on Amazon

Before you start publishing your first articles on Amazon, you must first know a few things.

Step 1: Start the buzz for the launch.

In the American version of "Queer as Folk," season 5 of episode 2 is about the reopening of the Babylon club by Brian. He knows it's hard to get his momentum, so he pays players to stand in line, so the club feels it's the hottest place in the block.

You will want to practice the same concept when you launch your product.

Do things like:

1. Write blog posts about the product so that buyers can access it once the product is published.
2. Set up social media so that potential buyers can spread the word. Create a hashtag and use it consistently, and watch it roll as a rollover while customers use it for themselves.
3. Post frequently and be thrilling about it. One of the worst things you may do is write tweets and updates that sound like a 90-year-antique robot has written them. Instead, do something like a thrilling reality of

sharing the day or grill your competition like Wendy's did with McDonald's.

Step 2: Make a list of all Kick-Ass products

Time is an enormous benefit when you start a product. You have days/weeks/months to perform the following tasks:

1. Take excellent high-resolution photos.
2. Shoot the product from a variety of angles.
3. Place it on a neutral-colored background so that it does not disturb the article itself.
4. Display the product of how it would be used in real life. Use natural sunlight to get the best possible lighting.
5. Write an informative description. If the photo initially attracts the buyer's attention, the written description can convince him to stay.
6. Describe why this product is an indispensable purchase with exciting promotional words.
7. Show (don't say) what is missing in their lives.
8. Search for similar products and see what other sellers have written, and they stood out.
9. Summarize by 3-5 points. If you have less than 3 points, you don't tell enough about the item. And if

you have more than five, you're going to be enlarged, and you can click on it.
10. Make sure you have some great keywords.
11. Again, searching is your best friend. Visit the competitors' sites to see what the most common keywords are and then use them in your own list.

Step 3: Collect many product reviews.

The launch of a new product is a bit of a trap: how to convince buyers to buy a product without notice, and how do you collect reviews for a product without a buyer?

Fortunately, you don't have to start Amazon first and delete the ratings.

Instead, first launch the product on your site, where you are fully responsible for all rules. Receive reviews from respected sources and post them on your site, then share your site on social media platforms and send buyers to your Amazon page.

From there, you can create reviews on your Amazon site because buyers find that you are a trusted seller.

Step 4: Provide a complete inventory

This may seem so clear, but you never want to make the mistake of not being in stock. First, it creates a lack of interest among buyers (why would they stay with you if you don't have what they want?). On the other hand, it can damage your reputation (will buyers tell other buyers to stay away from you because you have no items available and someone else has them?).

However, if you experience an unfortunate situation that is not in stock, you must choose between two basic strategies:

Increase the price to temporarily lower interest rates and lower the selling speed.

Reduce the price to drive more traffic to your site and hope that the exceeded volume disappoints.

Not being in stock is never a good thing, but it's up to you to see how you handle it.

Step 5: Launch

Chapter 8

What is Arbitrage?

Arbitrage is a practice that benefits from a price distinction between two or more markets where a mixture of matching agreements is established to help from the imbalance. The distinction between those market expenses is the income that has been determined by the individual bringing the operation together. The difference between these two market expenses is the earnings determined by the use of the character that brings the transaction together.

It just means you're going to find products that you can buy low and sell high. You can find the items you need to buy and sell for a profit. You're coordinating supply and demand.

Retail arbitration may also be referred to as resale, and those who buy resale products are referred to as resellers. These terms are used in this section as well.

Another significant difference that needs to be made when debating Retail Arbitration is the retail market and the price compared to the secondary market and the price. Stores are the primary market and are bound by price contracts with producers concerning rates that they may or may not charge. When supply and demand change rapidly, the prices in shops will not be impacted. What is affected is the capacity to buy these products at the sale price. If demand increases, you may not be able to locate them in shops or on the primary market because all the shops are empty.

In the secondary market, the price is determined solely by supply and demand. When the need for derivatives rises and the quantity for sale stays the same, the price on the secondary market rises. All this is a mere economy and human behavior. If the price on the secondary market is greater than the price charged in shops, entrepreneurs or resellers will join the market by purchasing a product at an artificially low retail price and making that offer on the secondary market when the cost is determined by high demand and the small supply is much greater.

From the arbitration definition: PROFIT is the gap between market prices.

When eBay began, a whole fresh idea was launched in the globe of retail arbitration. They had everyone wherever they were, to sell everything to someone.

This established an open secondary market in which the price was determined on the grounds of supply and demand. It was so open that prices often returned rapidly to the cost of balance. It's become so hard to discover something for a reduced cost than eBay. Retail Arbitration vendors long before you could sell on Amazon have discovered products to purchase and sell on eBay. If an item could be bought on eBay at a price lower than the market price, it would end up on eBay.

While eBay still offers some possibilities for Retail Arbitrage, as well as some approaches to sell at greater margins when Amazon prices and market conditions alter, this book is mostly about Retail Arbitrage using Amazon.com as your main marketing channel.

What is Retail Arbitrage?

When financial experts hear the term 'arbitrage,' they almost always immediately think of price movements. Traditional arbitrage happens when two or more currency prices are not suitable in the trading economy.

But arbitration must not be restricted to cash. You can discover it in the retail store. That's when you purchase a cheap product and sell it at a higher cost while maintaining the profit.

This is no different than the way a number of retail stores have always worked. Sellers purchase items at an auction, at wholesale prices, or at individual sellers. They then sell them to the public at a higher price.

What is different from retail arbitrage in modern times is democratization. You no longer need a physical store or even your own online sales site to sell items for profit. Successful retail arbitrators generally find cheap, discount, or liquidation items in their local savings or big box stores. They buy the shares and then post their finds online at a higher price.

Sites such as eBay, Craigslist, and even Amazon offer you the opportunity to sell directly to your potential customers. This can be an excellent way to dive into arbitration.

Retail arbitrage: buy, sell, and earn a passive income.

Retail arbitrage is not just about buying something with a discount and selling online. You must ensure that you identify quality products that will sell. Some things go into this:

Purchase the right products

You can make earnings on retail arbitrage with some different products. But it can be a bit of practice to identify a marketable product.

According to Renegade Resale, the four factors to look for when buying items in a store to sell online are potential income, quantity, size, and weight, as well as demand.

Other things to consider

Some additional rules can help a referee to benefit without a headache:

Make sure you find items that cost between $10 and $30. Less than $10, and your income margin is potentially minimal, even if you double your money. More than $ 30, and you are considering a sizeable initial expense if you want to buy wholesale.

Size and weight are important, and there is a reason why nobody wanted these Shakespeare anthologies: they were bulky and heavy. The shipping costs would have absorbed Even a considerable profit margin.

Consider fragility. Other potential shipping costs are related to the vulnerability of your sales item. You must pay for the package if you have to continue to ensure that it arrives at your buyer in one piece.

Limit your arbitration to items with a high rating. If you're trying to sell items with an average rating of one or two stars, you might be bothered for a while. If you are considering buying an item for arbitration, review the review pages to make sure it is not a malfunction.

Look for a decent profit margin that can handle price changes. Experts recommend striving for a profit margin of between 40% and 50%. This gives you the space to lower your price and make a profit if another seller offers the same item.

You can easily check the first three rules of thumb in the store, but the last two require some research from you. Plan your smartphone in the store to check Amazon reviews and the price of the item you are considering. Even if you don't intend to sell to Amazon, it can give you a good idea of what to expect.

From there, take the time to check your product on CamelCamelCamel, a site that maintains historical prices on Amazon. This can help you determine whether the product you are considering selling will be sold quickly and with profit.

Tips for Retail Arbitrage on eBay

So do you want to know how you can sell things on eBay, or do you want an eBay company? There is a huge difference between the two, you know.

Most people who "want to sell things" look in their attic or basement for items they don't use. Although I am not saying that this strategy does not work in the short term, this is not the way to build a business in the long term.

Sooner or later, you will miss things on the market; If you want a "business," you must continuously look for profitable products to get hold of the long term.

First of all, here is a strategy that few people talk about selling items on eBay: arbitration. Admittedly, arbitration is a well-known method.

On the stock market, you are looking for undervalued shares in certain markets. You then buy them, turn them around and release them in the market where they are overvalued. You only make a small profit with every sale, and the key to this activity is the large volume.

For example, if you see Microsoft's shares in Japan sell 2/8 of their price in Los Angeles, you would buy them and then immediately unload them in Los Angeles for profit. Arbitration is best known for its use on the stock market, but it can be used in many business models, including eBay.

Remember, this is a discount website, and things are cheaper than many other places. If you understand that an item is worth more than what it is presently selling on eBay, you can purchase and resell it on eBay with a stronger offer or elsewhere for more cash.

Elsewhere, your own website, the Craigslist newspaper, may mean, among others. The opposite is to buy items that sell offline for less and then sell them on eBay, which also works.

There is a lot of money to win with the referee, and if you play your cards well, you can earn a lot of money. Keep in mind, however, that this strategy requires a lot of risks and that you must be very useful in finding products that are unsold to be profitable. Otherwise, it can explode in the face.

Of course, there are other ways to sell items on eBay and generate a significant profit. Buying wholesale or depositing shipped items and then placing them on eBay is the one that gets the most attention, and that is what I would recommend in the long run.

How to sell on Amazon with Retail Arbitration

It is relatively easy to sell items via the Amazon website and the vast distribution network. They have a program called Fulfillment organized by Amazon (FBA) that allows you to ship your products directly to Amazon until they are sold. Have you ever noticed the different suppliers you can choose when you buy on Amazon? These are suppliers who use Amazon Fulfillment.

With Fulfillment by Amazon, you can send your items to Amazon cheaper. The store giant stores your items in their warehouse. Immediately a customer has made a purchase, he packs and ships your goods directly to the customer. Amazon even takes care of returns and customer service for orders.

The costs for using Fulfillment by Amazon depend on the number of items you sell, their size, how long they are stored in the warehouse, and whether or not you pay per item or a fixed amount.

If you sell fewer than 40 items per month, you pay a unit rate of $2.41 to $5.26 for standard-sized items — warehouse costs of $0.69/cubic foot from January to September and $2.40/cubic foot during the Christmas period.

These FBA costs may be worth it for the part-time retail arbitrator if you want to find great deals on items. Madison from My Dollar Plan uses this program and earned more than $ 10,000 in her free time in arbitration with Amazon last year. To increase her profit, she uses her cashback credit card to make purchases.

Chapter 9

How You Can Work From Home

Many experts would like to explain the benefits of working remotely, from home. For example, you make your schedule, earn a lot of money without "real work," and enjoy a lifestyle that allows you to travel anywhere, anytime.

But how many of them have you ever told how YOU can do it?

If you read this eBook, it is because you are wondering:

- ❏ How can I work at home if I have no experience?
- ❏ How can I earn enough money to replace my full-time job?
- ❏ Do I have to sell clothing, makeup, essential oils, or plastic to store food to have an income at home?

Do not worry if you have problems answering these questions. You are in the right place.

Working from home seems to be the dream of many people. Women, in particular, are attracted by the opportunity to earn money to take care of their families at the same time.

Time.

There are three ways to work at home:

- Direct marketing: sale of Avon, Tupperware, Mary Kay, spoiled chef, etc.
- Manage your own company
- As a permanent employee of a company

Direct marketing

Selling products to your family and friends, and their friends is a way to make money at home. The following website offers sales ideas for some of the largest companies.

To do this kind of work, you have to love selling and be highly motivated. No one will knock on your door to buy your product.

You need to know yourself and know if you can organize 'parties' and do the rest of the work required to make a profit. If you are shy and withdraw, this is not a task for you. You often have to do much work to earn your commission.

Manage your own business

By starting your business, you can continue and do something that you love. Because you are the boss, you can decide when you will or will not work.

Arranging family affairs can be more relaxed. The sources at the end of this article can provide you with some easy ideas for home affairs.

Remember the returns at home

The company is the measure of the time you spend. Don't expect to earn a lot of money if you don't spend a lot of time, especially in the beginning. Moreover, this is a rare home business that does not need time outside.

Work at Home Scams

We have to be careful! The National Consumer League lists the number seven vacancies on a home base among the ten internet fraudsters. Also, the Council of Better Business Agencies responded last year to more than one million investigations into such programs.

The common scams include medical billing, envelope filling, and processing of "unclaimed funds." Advertisements usually do not take into account the fact that you may have to work many hours without paying or state all the costs that you must pay. A lot of scams at work requires you to spend your money. There are legitimate opportunities online, but they are tough to find.

Work at home for a "real" company

There are legit opportunities to work at home as a "normal" employee. The internet has made telework possible for many employees. In general, however, an employee must have a proven work history before a company leaves employees to work at home. If a company knows that the employee is reliable and that homework can be done, some employers will allow telework.

Most telework is still part-time. Rare opportunities to work at home include an easily controlled workload. The most important thing is to have an excellent track record with an employer in a profession that can be transferred home.

Keep in mind that working at home leaves little time for family responsibilities.

Your employer expects you to work during the time he/she pays you, does not change diapers, or wears bathing shoes.

Tips For Working From Home

Whatever work you do at home, this book offers some suggestions to make it work.

- Balance priorities at both ends. Sometimes, to do the work or to meet the needs of the customer, the work must first come.
- Individual work and family obligations.
- Set a schedule and stick to it.
- Find shortcuts and group work/home tasks.
- Choose the type of work that is suitable for you: writing, illustrations, freelance work, data entry, telephone sales, etc.
- Hire a professional if you are not organized.
- Know that working from home is usually not a picnic

Working from home is not as easy as it appears on the surface. If you have previously worked outside the home, you may miss the interaction with your colleagues. Moreover, it is not for those who have low motivation. It will be challenging to find a balance between work and childcare. Of course, it is possible to manage the dream of working from home. Make sure you have what you need and do your homework!

Chapter 10

How to Get Into Real Estate

Investment services cover a wide range of categories. So many people wonder and would like to invest in properties, and some people choose it as a profession. The most important aspect of learning investment services is understanding many different facets of investing in real estate. You have a diversity of choices in this profession, and you can practice and specialize among them.

Let's talk about real estate investment services from the perspective of specialization in each of its facets. This area can be divided on the premise of various types of actual property for which investments may be made. We can subdivide the domain into the following main types:

- Pretty much
- Commercial real estate
- Homes - divided into two types:
- Single-family homes

- Multi-family homes

Some real estate investment professionals are very familiar with work in the wasteland and developing land. Others deliberately work with commercial real estate, and many of the real estate investment professionals specialize in residential property. Investors in this category invest their finances primarily in single-family and multi-family homes.

But which of these types is the best investment firm? This must be dealt with in detail here from my point of view. The answer is no longer doubtful to me; they are "single-family homes." But the dilemma is that investors do not consider single-family homes as an 'investment.' For example, you can go to the bank and borrow money to buy a multi-family complex with 200 units, but if you go to the same bank and try to borrow money to buy two or three houses where you are going to have a problem with that.

So if you were to ask me what you would say if I am having trouble borrowing banks to buy detached houses, why would that be a good investment for you? The reason is that most banks and people ignore single-family homes as investment opportunities. Let me explain why?

We can compare investments in single-family homes with each of the types, such as vacant plots or homes or multi-family homes. For example, if you look at commercial real estate, it is very easy to look at capitalization rates and analyze these properties on a larger scale, and there are many players. They want big projects, and they analyze them in competition for things like that. But if you're talking about single-family homes, looking for individual properties, and trying to find homes in good neighborhoods at low prices, look at the worst of the house. It takes more effort. They are difficult to define, and as a result, fewer people will attack them.

Single-family homes offer excellent investment opportunities due to the many available solutions. If you rent them, you can find excellent tenants who take care of the house, so you don't have to repair the property. There are only many opportunities. Today's topic is; The most significant investment opportunity for real estate lies in single-family homes in the more significant and thriving real estate investment company.

How to Make Passive Income With Real Estate

Do you want to know how to get into real estate? Well, there are, of course, compulsory courses and classes to be taught and licensed to start your career. But when all of this is done, then what? Yeah, you guessed it-years of trial and error learning and the slow and steady acquisition of know-how in the field.

So, why not latch onto somebody who has enjoyed the success that years of expertise will provide? We see these people from time to time, sailing through deals that no one ever knew existed, making deals that would seem to be lousy investment risks to beginners, and quickly collecting profits that would make anyone salivate with envy.

By the way, by increasing your know-how to get into real estate, go ahead and try to get some of their secrets out of it. It just doesn't happen, and can you blame them? If you were one of the seasoned field veterans, would you freely disclose your secrets to anyone? You'd tell your brand new, well-armed competition of all your hard-earned tips and trade tricks! So what's going to be done about this? How can we find a mentor who would be willing to share their wisdom on how best to get into real estate?

The fact is, there are those who share their knowledge, and the way they do it is through distance learning on the Internet.Learning this know-how online is a good way to share knowledge while not being competitive in every other's corner of the real estate world. Once you find a mentor who can help you improve on how to get into the already-competitive estate world, you'll learn about the obstacles without having to become their victim and all the sweet hidden deals without spending years in the business beforehand.

Conclusion

If you are talking about passive income, this is the average salary of the other contractor or employer. This type of income can come from a company in which a person does not actively participate. The best example is dividend-paying shares and royalties on books.

What are the different ideas for passive income?

It is quite challenging to think about generating passive income ideas, especially if you have no idea, and you are a newcomer to this type of business.

Invest in a credit club

It is a source of residual income that ensures that you earn a constant interest in your investments. Loan clubs offer you the opportunity to receive attention for years.

Do you have repayment incentives on your credit card?

If you use credit for your purchases, searching for credit card rewards is no problem. With most bonuses, you can effortlessly earn 1 to 5% of your money. If you utilize a credit card for your convenience, you'll be able to make a lot of money by signing up for an online bonus. At the same moment, you can also have a residual online revenue using this method.

Try index funds

Index funds are a type of investment fund that can be a means of investing in a stock market that generates a considerable amount of passive income.

Create money from what you do regularly

It is possible to earn money and generate passive income with what you already do regularly (gaming, data entry, etc.). There are so many examples in abundance where you can earn money while doing what you love most.

Invest in real estate

Investing in real estate is another sure way to generate residual income. This includes receiving an accumulated amount on a rented property.

In general, ideas about how to earn passive income are not as easy as it sounds, you will spend much time perfecting them.

www.ingramcontent.com/pod-product-compliance
Lightning Source LLC
Chambersburg PA
CBHW071405210526
45465CB00001B/255